MIRACLES
of Love

WHEN MIRACLES HAPPEN
True Stories of God's Divine Touch

Edited by Mary Hollingsworth

Guideposts Books
Carmel, New York

Acknowledgments

Every attempt has been made to credit the sources of copyrighted material used in this book. If any such acknowledgment has been inadvertently omitted or miscredited, receipt of such information would be appreciated.

All material that originally appeared in Guideposts publicatons is reprinted with permission. Copyright © Guideposts, Carmel, NY.

Scripture quotations marked (KJV) are taken from the *King James Version.*

Scripture quotations marked (RSV) are taken from the *Revised Standard Version* of the Bible, copyright © National Council of Churches of Christ in America. Used by permission.

Scripture quotations marked (NCV) are taken from *The Holy Bible*, New Century Version®, copyright © 1987, 1988, 1991 by Thomas Nelson, Inc. Used by permission.

Scripture quotations marked (NIV) are taken from *The Holy Bible*, New International Version. Copyright © 1973, 1978, 1984, International Bible Society. Used by permission of Zondervan Bible Publishers.

"Reckless Faith" by Katherine G. Bond, "The Nightlight" by Nancy Jo Eckerson, "A Sign" by Patti Maguire Armstrong, "A Half Hour Early" by Elizabeth Blake, "The Christmas Gift of Love" by Christine Trollinger, "If I Could Just Phone Home" by Elizabeth J. Schmeidler, "Is Eight Enough?" by Mark Armstrong, "Sometimes You Just Gotta Listen!" by Elizabeth J. Schmeidler, "A Voice from God" by Mary Hollingsworth, "The A Cappella Angel" by Mary Hollingsworth, "Pride Goeth Before a Water Ticket" by Elizabeth J. Schmeidler, "The Story of Daniel" by Christine Trollinger, "Hayden's Miracle" by Aimee Perrine, "Go Home, Now!" by Vicki P. Graham, "When I Stumble" by Vikki Denisi Hanson is from *Whispers from Heaven*, Publications International, LTD, used by permission. "The Changed Heart" by Mary Ann Kelly, "Right On Time" by Vicki P. Graham; are used by permission of the authors.

www.guideposts.org
(800) 431-2344
Guideposts Books & Inspirational Media Division

Typeset by Inside Out Design & Typesetting
Illustrations by Jim Haynes
Jacket design by The DesignWorks Group, Inc.
Photo by iStock.com

Printed in the United States of America

Contents

*C*HAPTER 1   LOVE'S DREAMS COME TRUE

*C*HAPTER 2   LOVE'S GREATEST TREASURE

*C*HAPTER 3 WHISPERS OF A FRIEND'S LOVE

*C*HAPTER 4 REACHING OUT IN LOVE

*C*HAPTER 5   LITTLE TAPS OF LOVE FROM HEAVEN

Introduction

Peple don't perform miracles; God does . . . in His own time, in His own way, in His great wisdom, and for our benefit.

True enough, sometimes God uses people as part of the miracle He's providing: it may come through a mate, a family member, a friend, or even a stranger. And while those people are broken vessels into which God pours His marvelous divine Spirit on a temporary basis, it is still God Himself who is the supernatural Being who makes them happen. Without Him there would be no miracles.

Why does God perform miracles? It's because He loves us so. In fact, He's crazy about us! And He wants us to be full of joy and hope. Sometimes His miracle relights the fire of a fading faith; sometimes it astounds medical personnel and helps them remember their ability to heal comes from Him; sometimes it creates a curiosity that leads a seeker to Him. But always and always it comes out of His great mercy and love for us.

Miracles of Love is a marvelous collection of stories

that show God's wonderful love through His miracles, both great and small, in the lives of people just like you and me. There simply can be no other explanation for the mysterious and amazing things that often happen in people's lives, as these heartwarming stories will reveal.

The romantic stories in chapter one, "Love's Dreams Come True," include the tale of a boy from the Jewish ghetto who is befriended by a young girl who throws him apples over the fence of the concentration camp where he's held captive. Love blooms between two strangers at the Camellia Grill. And two families are united by God when they meet, not so coincidentally, at McDonald's.

In chapter two, "Love's Greatest Treasure," God's love is shown through miracles with families as a woman is assured of her deceased mother's love when her nightlight flickers at just the right time in answer to her prayer. A policeman and his wife are blessed to learn that their son who died is happy in heaven. And baby Chloe is protected from being killed in an automobile accident by a hole in the ground *just her size.*

Miracles of friendship are described in chapter three, "Whispers of a Friend's Love," when Elizabeth is prompted by God to call her friend Laura, just at the precise moment Laura needs her. A professor announces God's unexpected plan for Mary's life that leads to an incredible career. And two girls from different backgrounds and with vastly different abilities become unlikely but fast friends.

Uncommon acts of kindness in chapter four, "Reaching Out in Love," show God's love through miracles between strangers in stories like the mysterious bus driver who just *happened* to be at the right place at the right time to rescue a whole Christian choir. Kindred hearts are bound together in love when an angel on her shoulder helps Darlene create a miracle. And a tiny baby with extensive physical deformities, astounds his family and the doctors . . . with God's help.

A whispered warning sent Vicki and Roger racing home, arriving just as their son Nik is hit by a car, as chapter five, "Little Taps of Love from Heaven," describes miracles by God's own hand. And Vikki learns that God is always there to pick her up and make her ever thankful, even when times are hard.

It's likely that you could write your own *Miracles of Love* stories to add to this moving collection, because all the stories in the book are true and from people just like you. They powerfully demonstrate that our God is a God of love, who wants to be involved in our everyday lives . . . if we just invite Him to participate. When we do, life is richer, fuller, abundant. In fact, it's . . . miraculous!

MARY HOLLINGSWORTH

MIRACLES
of Love

CHAPTER 1

Love's Dreams Come True

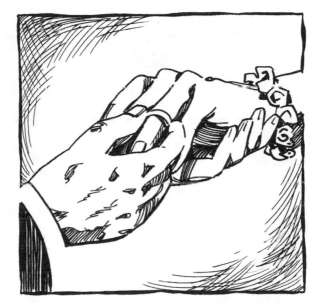

Even much water cannot put out the flame of love; floods cannot drown love. If a man offered everything in his house for love, people would totally reject it. (Song of Solomon 8:7, NCV)

L ove is a dream most of us have from the time we are
children. We dream of finding the perfect love—Mr.
Right or Miss Right. We hope for a romance and love that
will last a lifetime. With God's help, love's dreams come
true. Whether sooner or later, whether perfect or not,
whether fiery or comfortable, love comes softly and often
on the wings of a miracle from God.

The Girl with the Apple

HERMAN ROSENBLAT

August, 1942. Piotrkow, Poland. The sky was gloomy that morning as we waited anxiously. All the men, women, and children of Piotrkow's Jewish ghetto had been herded into a square. Word had gotten around that we were being moved. My father had only recently died from typhus, which had run rampant through the crowded ghetto. My greatest fear was that our family would be separated. "Whatever you do," Isidore, my eldest brother, whispered to me, "don't tell them your age. Say you're sixteen." I was tall for a boy of eleven, so I could pull it off. That way I might be deemed valuable as a worker. An SS man approached me, boots clicking against the cobblestones. He looked me up and down, then asked my age. "Sixteen," I said. He directed me to the left, where my three brothers and other healthy young men already stood.

My mother was motioned to the right—with the other women, children, sick, and elderly people. I whispered to Isidore, "Why?" He didn't answer. I ran to Mama's side and said I wanted to stay with her. "No," she said sternly. "Get away. Don't be a nuisance. Go with your brothers." She had never spoken so harshly before. But I understood: she was protecting me. She loved me so much that, just this once, she pretended not to. It was the last I ever saw of her.

My brothers and I were transported in a cattle car to Germany. We arrived at the Buchenwald Concentration Camp one night weeks later and were led into a crowded barracks. The next day, we were issued uniforms and identification numbers. "Don't call me Herman anymore," I said to my brothers. "Call me 94983." I was put to work in the camp's crematorium, loading the dead onto a hand-cranked elevator. I, too, felt dead. Hardened. I had become a number.

Soon, my brothers and I were sent to Schlieben, one of Buchenwald's subcamps near Berlin. One morning I thought I heard my mother's voice. Son, she said softly but clearly, I am sending you an angel. Then I woke up. Just a dream. A beautiful dream. But in this place there could be no angels. There was only work. And hunger. And fear.

A couple of days later, I was walking around the camp, behind the barracks, near the barbed-wire fence where the guards could not easily see. I was alone. On the other side of the fence, I spotted someone—a young girl with light, almost luminous curls. She was half-hidden behind a birch tree. I glanced around to make sure no one saw me. I called to her softly in German, "Do you have something to eat?" She didn't understand. I inched closer to the fence and repeated the question in Polish. She stepped forward. I was thin and gaunt, with rags wrapped around my feet, but the girl looked unafraid. In her eyes, I saw life. She pulled an apple from her woolen jacket and threw it over the fence. I grabbed the fruit and, as I started to run away, I heard her say faintly, "I'll see you tomorrow."

I didn't believe she would come back. It was much too dangerous. But I returned anyway, the same time the next day. And there she was. The same girl. She moved tentatively from behind the tree, and once again threw something over the fence. This time, a small hunk of bread wrapped around a stone. I ate the bread, gratefully and ravenously, wishing there had been enough to share with my brothers. When I looked up the girl was gone.

I returned to the same spot by the fence at the same time every day. She was always there with something for me to eat—a hunk of bread or, better yet, an apple. We didn't dare speak or linger. To be caught would mean death for us both. I didn't know anything about her— just a kind farm girl—except that she understood Polish. What was her name? Why was she risking her life for me? Hope was in such short supply, and this girl on the other side of the fence gave me some, as nourishing in its way as the bread and apples.

Nearly seven months later, my brothers and I were crammed into a coal car and shipped to the Theresienstadt Camp in Czechoslovakia. "Don't return," I told the girl that day. "We're leaving." I turned toward the barracks and didn't look back, didn't even say good-bye to the girl whose name I'd never learned, the girl with the apples.

We were at Theresienstadt for three months. The war was winding down and Allied forces were closing in, yet my fate seemed sealed. On May 10, 1945, I was scheduled to die in the gas chamber at 10:00 A.M. In the quiet of dawn, I tried to prepare myself. So many times death seemed ready to claim me, but somehow I'd survived. Now, it was over. I thought of my parents. At least, I thought, we will be reunited. At 8:00 A.M., there was a commotion. I heard shouts, and saw people running every which way through camp. I caught up with my brothers. Russian troops had liberated the camp! The gates swung open. Everyone was running, so I did too. Amazingly, all of my brothers had survived; I'm not sure how. But I knew that the girl with the apples had been the key to my survival. In a place where evil seemed triumphant, one person's goodness had saved my life, had given me hope in a place where there was none. My mother had promised to send me an angel, and the angel had come.

Eventually, I made my way to England, where I was sponsored by a Jewish charity, put up in a hostel with other boys who had survived the Holocaust, and trained in electronics. Then I came to America, where my brother Sam had already moved. I served in the U.S. Army during the Korean War, and returned to New York City after two years. By August 1957 I'd opened my own electronics repair shop. I was starting to settle in.

One day, my friend Sid—whom I knew from England—called me. "I've got a date. She's got a Polish friend. Let's double date."

A blind date? Nah, that wasn't for me. But Sid kept pestering me, and a few days later we headed up to the Bronx to pick up his date and her friend Roma. I had to admit, for a blind date this wasn't so bad. Roma was a nurse at a Bronx hospital. She was kind and smart. Beautiful, too, with swirling brown curls and green, almond-shaped eyes that sparkled with life.

The four of us drove out to Coney Island. Roma was easy to talk to, easy to be with. Turned out she was wary of blind dates too! We were both just doing our friends a favor. We took a stroll on the boardwalk, enjoying the salty Atlantic breeze, and then had dinner by the shore. I couldn't remember having a better time.

We piled back into Sid's car, Roma and I sharing the backseat. As European Jews who had survived the war, we were aware that much had been left unsaid between us. She broached the subject. "Where were you," she asked softly, "during the war?"

"The camps," I said, the terrible memories still

vivid, the irreparable loss. I had tried to forget. But you never forget.

She nodded. "My family was hiding on a farm in Germany, not far from Berlin," she told me. "My father knew a priest, and he got us Aryan papers." I imagined how she must have suffered too—fear, a constant companion. And yet here we were, both survivors, in a new world. "There was a camp next to the farm," Roma continued. "I saw a boy there, and I would throw him apples every day."

What an amazing coincidence that she had helped some other boy. "What did he look like?" I asked.

"He was tall. Skinny. Hungry. I must have seen him every day for six months."

My heart was racing. I couldn't believe it . . . this couldn't be . . . "Did he tell you one day not to come back because he was leaving Schlieben?"

Roma looked at me in amazement. "Yes."

"That was me!" I was ready to burst with joy and awe, flooded with emotions. I couldn't believe it. My angel. "I'm not letting you go," I said to Roma. And in the back of the car on that blind date, I proposed to her. I didn't want to wait.

"You're crazy!" she said. But she invited me to meet her parents for Shabbat dinner the following week. There was so much I looked forward to learning about Roma, but the most important things I always knew:

her steadfastness, her goodness. For many months, in the worst of circumstances, she had come to the fence and given me hope. Now that I'd found her again, I could never let her go.

That day, she said yes. And I kept my word: after nearly fifty years of marriage, two children and three grandchildren, I have never let her go.

Reckless Faith

KATHERINE G. BOND

You think New Testament will be easy," Dr. Robert Wall glowered at us. "It won't be."

I disliked him immediately. How presumptuous! I worked for my grades. Certainly, I'd give a Bible class due diligence.

I was determined to excel at Seattle Pacific University. But I was faced with a major distraction. Andy.

We'd met when I was sixteen. Now I was nineteen and counting the months to our fall wedding.

"Marriage is risky business," worried folk admonished. "The divorce rate is 50 percent. Early marriage is reckless."

Reckless or not, I had found my soul mate. I longed to be with him. And after two and a half years my virginity was wearing thin.

But these were frivolous reasons. We wanted to be reverent and deliberate. We made an academic study of marriage, undertaking classes, counseling, stacks of books. But deep down I wondered if God could approve something so foolish.

Each morning I argued theology with Dr. Wall. To my surprise he responded thoughtfully. And as I learned about synoptics and exegetics, I began to respect him deeply.

"I believe," he said, "but I could be wrong. That's what faith is."

He was declaring faith to be more than intellectual calisthenics, challenging me to risk.

The term paper was "What It Means to Be a Christian."

"I don't want bibliographies," said Dr. Wall. "I want you to lie on your bed and think about this question. I grade on a scale of one to ten," he went on, "and only God gets a ten."

I prickled with the injustice of this, but I had other things to worry about. Money was scarce. A fall marriage now looked impossible. Reluctantly, we postponed the wedding by a year. It was obviously God's will.

I poured my heart into my paper. I spoke of my quest for humility, my failures. Perhaps I was too honest.

I had to chuckle at my score: "Ten-minus." But the comments took me straight to Dr. Wall's office.

"You don't like your grade?" he demanded.

"No. It's not that. I wanted to discuss the . . . theological implications of your notes."

I bumbled around, avoiding my real question. Finally, I turned to the section on God's will. I had used my deferred wedding as an example.

"It's what God seems to be leading us to," I wrote.

And Dr. Wall's scrawl in the margin responded, "Because it's *logical? God is transcendent!*"

"About this comment . . ." I attempted an aura of scholarly indifference.

Dr. Wall's face softened. "God can overcome circumstances," he said. "Perhaps you and your fiancé owe it to yourselves to rethink this decision."

My heart leapt. What a rash idea! Was he suggesting that God wanted what I wanted? Even so frivolous a thing as love?

Five months later I dropped a handmade wedding invitation on Dr. Wall's desk. "You're right," I wrote inside. "God is transcendent."

At the Camellia Grill

CLARE BIEDENHARN

I was driving around uptown New Orleans, trying to find a place to park. A summer breeze blew through the moss hanging from the old live oak trees. A half-empty streetcar rumbled by.

I was edgy. As part of the executive training program at the Maison Blanche department store I had to take a series of night classes, and my final exam was coming up. During the day I worked on the sales floor and helped out in the warehouse. It was a good job, and at the age of twenty-three I was having fun learning the ins and outs of the business. Coming from a tiny town in Indiana, I had fallen in love with the Big Easy, Dixieland jazz, the muddy Mississippi, the French Quarter. Something was always happening. Life never stopped in New Orleans.

Unfortunately, though, my social life was at a standstill. One guy I really liked hadn't called since he'd become immersed in premed classes. I'd gone out a couple of times with another fellow who, I later discovered, had conveniently forgotten to wear his wedding ring. When I found out, I showed him the door and slammed it behind him. Better to be alone, I thought, even if it means being lonely. At least I had the charms of the city to keep me company.

My plan that night was to splurge at a health-food restaurant on Prytania Street, then go home and study for my final. I drove around the block several times. No one pulled out. I wanted to have a nice dinner, but where?

As I headed down St. Charles toward Carrollton, I remembered the Camellia Grill. It was a venerable New Orleans establishment. With only counter service, the coffee shop usually had a line that went out the door and down the block. It reminded me of an old-fashioned tearoom. Pink cloth napkins, and Harry the bald waiter to chaperone. Mom would approve, I said to myself, thinking of how she worried about me.

There's probably no place to park here either, I thought as I drove by. Then a spot opened up right in front of the Camellia Grill. There was just enough room for my '74 Chevy. I parked and went inside.

It was a slow night, a Wednesday evening during the last week of July. The regular dinner crowd had come and gone. I sat and perused the menu.

"A glass of water," I told the waiter. (Harry wasn't working that night.) "And a bowl of vegetable soup."

Just as I sipped at the first spoonful, a tall, slim,

handsome man strolled in. He had thick, dark hair and brown eyes. With his horn-rimmed glasses and seersucker suit, he reminded me of Gregory Peck in *To Kill a Mockingbird*, except younger. The spoon froze in front of my lips. *Stop staring!* I told myself. Flustered, I looked away, hoping he hadn't caught me gazing at him.

Out of the corner of my eye I noticed him hesitate for a moment. There was an attractive girl sitting across the restaurant, and I figured he was going to sit by her. *Good*, I thought. *I shouldn't talk to strangers.* But the next thing I knew he was walking toward me. He sat on the stool one away from mine and ordered a cup of coffee. What was I to do?

I could hear my mother's warning: a young woman should never initiate a conversation with a strange man. Mother was absolutely right.

Then again, this was the Camellia Grill, about as wholesome a place as you could find in the Big Easy. And somehow this stranger in his seersucker suit seemed every bit as upstanding as Atticus Finch.

Then an amazing thing happened. I heard a voice from somewhere deep inside of me—it wasn't from anyone in the restaurant—and it was as clear as day. I couldn't ignore it: *if you don't talk to this guy, you are going to miss out on something really good.*

So what am I supposed to say? I wondered. *If this is such a big deal, what am I supposed to do?* I tried to remember every article I'd ever read about "101 Ways to Start a Conversation." My mind raced. Ask him what time it was? Comment on the steamy weather? All the possibilities seemed incredibly corny. Sitting on that stool, I could do nothing but pray. *God, if this really is a good idea, give me something to say.*

I sneaked a peek at the stranger again, at his long fingers wrapped around the coffee cup. Then it came to me.

"Could I have a cup of coffee, please?" I asked the waiter. New Orleans coffee with chicory is strong enough to peel paint, and drinking it seemed to separate the natives from the hicks like me. I doctored mine with cream and sugar. I took a swig and winced—it might as well have been a shot of whiskey. Setting the cup on its saucer, I said, as nonchalantly as possible, "Boy, this coffee is strong, isn't it?"

"Sure is," the stranger drawled in a Delta accent as distinctive as the coffee. He smiled and ordered a refill. "Where y'all from?"

"Not from around here," I said.

"Me neither."

A silence filled the pause—but something filled the silence: a warmth, a stilling of time, as if the stool and the space between us didn't exist. It was a feeling I will never forget.

Many months later I found out he'd been lonely too. That he had gotten on his knees two nights earlier and prayed to find someone to help him feel at home in the Big Easy. But that evening what I learned was that he had recently moved from Vicksburg, Mississippi, to take a new job. His name was James, and he was living by himself and hadn't made any friends since he'd arrived.

We talked so long that the waiter stopped refilling our cups and started cleaning the counter, but James and I were completely absorbed in each other and didn't get the hint. Finally I realized I still needed to study for my final, so we stood and paid our bills. Out in front of the restaurant on that warm summer evening we both lingered on the sidewalk, trying to keep the conversation from ending. I heard the horns of the boats on the river and the bell of the streetcar as it passed. I looked into James's eyes, shining in the light of a streetlamp. Finally he said, "I enjoyed this so much I'd like to talk to you again. May I call you?"

"Please do," I said.

All this happened more than twenty years ago, and I can confess to only a few other times in my life when I have felt so completely and surely guided to take a course of action. Such a time came ten years later when I saw an announcement outside of a Kroger's grocery store about a Methodist church gathering in a tiny Tennessee town; we went, and it became our community. Or when the spirit in that church inspired half a dozen men to enter the ministry, and James followed as the seventh.

As you can probably guess, James became my husband, and although his hair is no longer as thick or as brown, he still looks every bit as handsome to me as on that night at the Camellia Grill. And when we sit down to breakfast with our two sons, we always start our day with a good cup of coffee. I make it with chicory and, yes, it is very strong.

When Marriage Destroys Love

DELLA DOWNING

I do not use my real name because I do not wish my husband to know about the ugly battle I have had to fight out all alone within myself. I am going to tell our story because I think other wives may recognize parts of it, may see where I failed as a wife and even, if I can express it right, see how prayer gave me back my husband.

Hank and I started our marriage with hope and willingness and love. Looking back, I think our trouble began when the children started coming, so close together. For some reason having babies was harder for me than it had been for Hank's mother or his three sisters.

For the nine months before each birth I was utterly miserable, and for nearly as long afterward I hardly had the strength to see to the baby. The apartment, Hank's meals, everything else just got neglected.

Then our third child was born two months early. For those first four months she had to be fed every two hours, around the clock. Everything we wore when we picked her up, everything that touched her, had to be boiled.

Everything was a struggle for her. If Jimmy or Gloria got sniffles, with Margot it became a life-and-death battle to keep the infection from the lungs and kidneys. Not once during those three years did Hank and I get thoroughly, completely rested. The other children were just babies themselves; Jimmy was under a year when Margot was born, Gloria just two and not a good sleeper. Deadly habit kept us going. Each one took care of his duties and largely ignored the other. We were too tired for much else.

And in this constricted existence, a tragic and terrifying thing happened: we began to turn on each other. We began to look for things to criticize. I discovered that there was a history of premature births in Hank's family, and I made the most of it. I asked if he was ever going to get a raise. He said I complained every time the sun didn't shine. (I did, but the truth hurts no less than falsehood. Maybe it hurts more.)

It doesn't take much of this attack and counter-attack to set up the habit of quarreling. What had begun simply as monotony and physical weariness had become, by the seventh year of our marriage, contempt and even hatred—shrill and outspoken.

One morning after Hank had slammed from the

apartment, I was sobbing at the kitchen table when there was a knock at the door; it was the lady from the next apartment. "I wasn't eavesdropping," she said, "but I couldn't help hearing. Are you in trouble?"

Mrs. White hadn't lived next door long. She was maybe sixty or sixty-five and looked just enough like my mother that suddenly I wanted to talk to her.

"You don't know him!" I said. "I hate him and I'm leaving him."

Mrs. White said not a word. She sat down and just let me rave, for nearly an hour, spitting out all the things I hated in Hank, his sarcasm, his "marvelous" family, his sloppiness. "He'd never shave if I didn't yell at him."

When it was all said, she looked at me with her gentle blue eyes. "And you didn't notice any of these things when you married him?"

"He was different then! He's not at all like the man I married!"

Still very gently, "Are you the girl he married?"

Even as my face grew hot, I knew the answer. I looked down at the bathrobe with the pablum caked down the front. When had I stopped wearing lipstick? When had the whine crept into my voice?

During the next few months I made a prodigious effort to change. I kept the apartment neater. I tried new recipes. The hardest thing was being sweet and forbearing with Hank, but I forced myself to do it.

It had no effect on him whatsoever, except to drive him to new heights of sarcasm.

It got so I lived for Mrs. White's visits. I would reel off for her the marvelous things I had done and the extent of Hank's ingratitude. She never said much.

Then one morning—it was just after New Year's, 1953—I was telling her about dinner the night before. "I even had candles on the table, and you know what he said? He said, 'What woman's magazine did you read that in?' He didn't even. . ."

"Della!" It was the first time Mrs. White had interrupted me. "Hank doesn't sound to me like a man who needs candles with his dinner; he sounds to me like a man who needs love."

For a long moment the apartment was perfectly silent. "Why," I stammered at last, "that's what this is all about, isn't it? I mean, fixing myself up, keeping the apartment clean, not quarreling."

But it wasn't, and suddenly I knew it. Suddenly I knew that love hadn't entered into it at all. I'd gone through the outward motions without touching the bitterness inside me. And, of course, a show of love, without the real thing, is powerless.

Real love must come from inside, welling up in the heart first, and only then spilling out in actions and words.

"But I need a little love too!" I told Mrs. White.

"Why Della," she said. "God loves you! Go to Him in prayer."

To Mrs. White it was a very simple thing: pray and God would answer. For someone like her, with an established and disciplined prayer life, this might have worked. But I was new and awkward at prayer. My first fumbling attempts were all on the order of, "Dear God, please change Hank so I can love him." Hank, of course, stayed as he was.

"It just isn't fair!" I told Mrs. White after several weeks of waiting for a reforming thunderbolt from heaven. "Why should I have to do all the changing?

"You're still blaming him, aren't you? Would you hate a wounded animal," she asked, "if it snapped at you while you cleaned its wound? Hank was wounded, I'm guessing, very deeply, when the children took your time and love away from him."

Suddenly, for the first time, I saw Hank as a victim, like myself, of difficult circumstances. That night my prayer was different: "Dear God, help me to see Hank as You see him."

Well, it wasn't easy. At first I despaired of finding even one good thing. But Friday, when he tossed his paycheck onto the table, instead of the usual sinking feeling: "How can I stretch it out to last the week?" I found myself thinking instead: "Hank brings every cent he earns home to me and the children! He doesn't keep out a dime for himself."

For days I silently wrapped Hank in that thought and used it to push away negative, angry feelings. Gradually it got easier. Soon I was noticing his very real affection for the children, especially Jimmy. I said none of it out loud and yet, did I imagine it or was there a new look, half doubting, half hopeful, in Hank's eyes?

Meanwhile, though, I was making another discovery, a discovery about prayer itself. How can I express it? Prayer made me feel good: that was all, really. No matter what demand I made of God, the answer was always a glow in my heart, an indescribable feeling of being warmed and cared for. Now I stopped asking. I stopped specifying just what wonder God was to perform in my life, and simply let myself relax in this new and all-sufficient relationship.

As I grew more practiced in prayer, I could lift myself wordlessly to God's presence. Then I would be so rewarded with love and joy and peace that these things just seemed to spill over from me to Hank and the children.

I don't mean that I was miraculously changed into some kind of all-suffering saint. The miracles were small, everyday ones. The business of Hank's shaving for instance. I'd tried every way I knew to get him to shave and only succeeded in starting fresh quarrels. Now one morning I heard myself saying, really meaning it, "Darling, even with that fuzz you're the best looking man I know!" Hank stared at me, then his hand went to his chin. "Golly. Didn't know I looked so frowsy." He raced for his razor and has shaved daily ever since.

A little thing, but oh, what a big lesson for me! Love—real love—had done in an instant what months of contriving could never do. Time was on our side, too, to be perfectly accurate. That spring the doctor pronounced Margot a pint-sized but normal three-year-old. Was it time alone though, or did the changed atmosphere in our home have anything to do with it? Love cures so many ills, so many problems.

And all of us can have this love—just for the taking. I know that when Mrs. White first told me, "God loves you," they were just so many words to me, and pretty vague and empty words too. Yet now, if an unhappy wife should ask me, "How can I bring love into our lives?" I wouldn't know how else to put it. God loves us, and prayer is how we let ourselves know it.

The Woman Who Couldn't Cry

SUSAN HOLLIDAY BEAUDRY

By the time I turned twenty-two, I was pretty much of a snob. I was mainly interested in good times. Appearances meant a great deal to me. In evaluating possible dates, I can remember confiding to my friends, "He's not tall enough," or, "I don't like the color of his hair—blonds are my type." My boyfriends also had to be athletic because I was crazy about sports. A new bowling ball was helping me edge up toward a two hundred game. In high school I played on a girls' football team.

The pace of my life accelerated after I finished school. Knowing I'd get bored sitting behind a desk in an office, I took a job in an aircraft factory. I was on my feet all day helping the mechanics, and I loved it. My spare time was devoted to whirling around dance floors, watching ball games played by my company teams on weekends, and vacationing in Europe.

I went to church, too, but that was mostly because I had gotten into the habit and liked to be around the other young people who also attended.

One Sunday morning in June 1969, I walked out of my apartment, climbed into my car, buckled my seat belt, and headed for church. I really don't remember getting into the car, however. I don't even remember going to bed the night before.

My knowledge of the events of that day comes from my family and newspaper accounts I read later. I was driving toward the Boulevard Park Presbyterian Church, a half mile away from my apartment. As I went through an intersection, a car driven by another young woman sped toward me. I had the right of way, but that was little consolation for what happened next. The other driver slammed into me broadside on the passenger's side. I was wrenched from under the seat belt and thrown free of the car into a rocky wall on the side of the road.

For the next three and a half months I was in a coma. Suffering from multiple fractures and internal bleeding, I needed electric shocks to keep my heart beating, and in one day I received a transfusion of eleven pints of blood.

"If Susan does live," the doctors told my parents, "you should be prepared to see considerable brain damage." At best, they suggested, I would likely be a physical cripple and mental vegetable.

But I guess God had other ideas. For some medically

unexplained reason, I pulled out of the coma mentally alert. But even though my mental powers were intact, my body had undergone a radical change. I had lost about forty pounds, I couldn't speak, and I was unable to stop my legs from involuntarily thrashing against the hospital-bed railings.

For several days I kept thinking that I must be having a long nightmare—that I'd soon wake up and find I was the same old Susan Holliday. Then I'd blink and blink again, but the white hospital room would still be there.

Screams of frustration welled up inside me. *I've got to say something or even moan or grunt!* I'd think as I strained my throat and moved my lips. But no sound came out.

A month of desperately attempting to mutter just one syllable passed, and the maddening silence still held me. The doctors were pessimistic; they told me that because of damage to my vocal cords, I probably would never speak again.

Emotionally and physically drained, I finally decided to try prayer. Then I discovered that I didn't know how to talk with God. I fell back on an example I remembered from the Bible. All day long I repeated in my mind the first two words of Psalm 12: "Help, Lord . . . Help, Lord . . . Help, Lord . . ."

Dozens, hundreds of times that day I turned those words over in my thoughts. Finally, that very evening,

God responded. As I sat outside my room in my wheelchair, I saw my doctor at the nearby nurses' desk and I
somehow softly rasped my first words in more than
four months, "Hello, Doctor Nelson."

From that wonderful moment on, the incredible
power of simple prayer became an everyday reality to
me. Hardly an hour went by when I didn't talk to God
about something.

As I slowly learned to speak again, I found my vocal
cords wouldn't always work. The words were there in
my head, but by the time they had passed through my
throat to my lips, the sound was often an unintelligible,
slurred croak or grunt. And because I could only manage one monotoned syllable for each breath, it was hard
to find anyone with enough patience and imagination to
sit around and absorb what I was trying to say.

Friends from my church and members of my family
did their best to communicate with me. But of them all,
John Beaudry, a young man I'd known slightly from my
high-school days, became my most concerned and
understanding companion. He surprised everyone by
continuing to visit me almost every day. He'd come into
the room and, like a big friendly bear, plant a brotherly
kiss on my forehead. Then he'd say quietly, "How're
you feeling?"

Although I usually had to repeat each sentence several times to others, John seemed to comprehend every-

thing immediately. We talked about trivial things—I can't even remember most of the conversations. But I can recall clearly how those tender, brown eyes of his would search my face.

In a way he seemed almost unaware of the seriousness of my injuries; he made it clear he regarded them as temporary problems. It was always, "When you go back to work . . ." or, "After you get back on your feet again . . ." His confidence in my recovery was infectious, and I began to find myself thinking the same way.

For some reason I couldn't explain at the time, I began to look forward to our comfortable visits more eagerly than any party or athletic event I had known before my accident. Still, I wasn't prepared for his words one afternoon soon after my late November discharge from the hospital. He came into my room at home and, looking very serious, said, "I love you, Susan, and I want to marry you."

My ears started ringing, and I caught my breath and shut my eyes. He had never hinted at romance. Except for those little pecks on the forehead, he'd never even kissed me. For a few moments I was silent as conflicting thoughts rushed in and out of my mind. More than anything else, I had always wanted to get married; but since the accident a gnawing feeling had made me doubt whether any suitable young man would ever want to take responsibility for someone with injuries and disabilities like mine.

Confused and upset, I responded lamely, "I can't be sure right now, John. Give me some time to think."

Thinking—and praying—became my primary occupation during the next two weeks. The accident may have changed me on the outside, but God was changing me even more radically on the inside. Even if I had wanted to, I knew I could no longer judge a person by his face or hair color. John's loving nature obviously made him someone special.

Finally I said yes. Then things began to happen so fast that I could hardly keep pace with them. Strength slowly returned to my weakened arms and back as physical therapy taught me to roll over, sit up, and crawl. And as summer approached, all my attention turned to preparations for the wedding.

Our church was packed that July day in 1970 when my dad rolled me down the aisle in my wheelchair. It was a beautiful wedding, and a lot of eyes were wet— but not mine. You see, another side effect of my accident was that something had gone wrong with my tear ducts. I couldn't cry.

And as I embarked on my challenging but frequently frustrating new career as a handicapped housewife, I often wished I could fall back on the emotional release that tears can provide.

One day not long after we were married I was sitting by the stove watching some meat simmer when I suddenly realized I had forgotten to add a sauce. I unlocked the brakes on my wheelchair, tediously wheeled myself to a cupboard, locked the brakes again and then, shakily, stood to get the sauce.

Then I slowly reversed the routine to get back to the stove, hoping all the time that the meat hadn't burned. At the same time a pot of water started boiling over and yet I could only watch it helplessly as I struggled, with rising despair, to position my wheelchair in front of the stove again.

Peeling a potato sometimes took five minutes or more—peel, pause, peel, pause, pick up the dropped potato. Cleaning our house was an even more humbling experience. I would slide to the floor from my wheelchair and crawl as well as I could, dragging the vacuum cleaner behind me.

Making the bed was another major project. Sometimes I'd collapse into a heap on the floor, overwhelmed with my physical handicaps. Unable to cry, I could feel the emotions boiling up inside until I thought I was about ready to explode.

But God was always there, and He supported me and relieved my anxieties when I prayed: "Lord, I'm so frustrated! Please help me. Give me a sense of peace, a confidence that Your will is being done in my life."

John's faith helped me too. As he watched me try to bring a bowl of salad to the table one evening in my wheelchair, I could see he was quietly confident that I was eventually going to make it. I had dropped the bowl before, and he knew I might drop it again. But he didn't pity me. He had the wisdom to be just firm enough to make me try to do things on my own instead of trying to do everything for me.

After I had placed the bowl carefully on the table, he said, "I knew you could do it." The affectionate look in those brown eyes—the eyes I had thought would have to be blue—helped me understand how deeply he loved me despite my physical limitations. It gave me the incentive to try to clear the next obstacle, and the next, and the next.

Gradually strength and flexibility began to return to my legs and increase in my arms. I found that I could hobble along haltingly behind a walker, then walk by leaning against a wall for support. Before long, I was able to carry large bowls with both my hands.

But most wondrous of all, despite the predictions of medical experts that I could never become pregnant, I did.

Our daughter, Janine, was born a year and a half after our marriage, and not even the painful pregnancy I endured could cast a shadow over the joy I felt when I looked into her sparkling blue eyes and fondled her soft hair. As I was recuperating from the delivery, John gave me a little book called, *How Much I Love My Wife*. The sense of my blessings overwhelmed me as I sat there holding that volume. And suddenly, for the first time in more than two years, I cried—not tears of frustration, but tears of total joy.

I know now that the car accident that I thought had ended my life was the best thing that has ever happened to me. I'm a different person—and all the changes have been for the better. Whenever I start to get blue, I think about the miracles God has performed in my life. I'm alive, I'm speaking much better, and I'm very much in love with the father of our own beautiful daughter. I seldom need a wheelchair or any other support to walk, and I see marked improvements in my condition almost every day.

All of that has been the result of trusting prayer. I truly have cause to shout Psalm 40:5 (RSV): "Thou hast multiplied, O LORD my God, thy wondrous deeds and thy thoughts toward us; none can compare with thee!"

Without Knowing Why

SHIRLEY AND TERRY LAW

Shirley's story:

The orange juice was already poured, the oatmeal nearly cooked, and I was stirring the scrambled eggs, when the crazy thought popped into my mind.

Take the kids to breakfast at McDonald's.

At first I ignored it. I'd been warned by other young widows that your mind plays tricks on you, living alone. I hadn't really been alone since my husband's death in April 1984, six months earlier—but the children were only six and four.

Go to McDonald's.

The thought came more urgently, and for a second I wondered if I was cracking up. But surely the time for that would have been those two-and-a-half years of watching my tall, blond, athletic young husband die inch by inch of a brain tumor.

If grief hadn't been able to destroy my sanity, I thought, mainly to keep my mind off this silly McDonald's notion, *money worries might have*. Jim had been a stockbroker here in Tulsa, Oklahoma, operating on commission, which stopped when he could no longer work.

I'd found a job selling Visa and MasterCard service to Tulsa businesses. It kept me out in the car a lot, and I'd cried a lot, there in the car. If I'd been going to fall apart, that would surely have been the time, with everything seemingly against us. Even the washing machine broke down, with no money to repair it, so that in the evening after working and cooking and caring for Jim and mowing the lawn, I'd have to drive out to the Laundromat.

Without faith in God, I thought as I gave the eggs a final turn, *I really might have gone crazy.* I'd carried a Bible in the car; when I felt panic rise I'd pull over and read and pray until I could go on.

The oatmeal was ready too. In the living room the kids were watching the Saturday morning cartoons. "Marie! Jason!" I called. "Wash your hands and come to the table."

And still something inside my head, quite independent of my own thoughts, was insisting that we were to leave this good hot meal right where it was, get in the car and drive a mile away to a fast-food outlet. I'd never in my life eaten breakfast at McDonald's! Where could such a notion be coming from?

Where indeed . . . ? From the bathroom I heard Marie and Jason splashing water on the floor. I stood there at the stove, spatula in hand, thinking back to a chilly

December day almost two years before. Wondering if the nudging in my head now was in any way like the nudging that had come to me then . . .

For a week I had been giving Jim and the children cold cereal because the stove, like the washing machine, had broken down, and Jim could no longer trust himself to try electrical repairs. We were three months behind on the house payments, and as for Christmas—Santa just wasn't going to find our chimney.

All that winter morning I had called on potential clients without success. As always when our situation threatened to overwhelm me, I'd pulled the car to the side of the road. And there God spoke to me as clearly as though He'd used audible words: *Will you trust Me, Shirley? For Jim, for the children, now and forever?*

I wanted to—oh, how I wanted to! But where could I get that kind of faith? Certainly I couldn't work it up on my own. "Father," I whispered, "give me that trust."

At once a kind of peace seemed to enter the car. And into that peace dropped the names of three local restaurants. I called on all of them that afternoon and signed on three new accounts.

From then on, these "impressions" came often, sometimes about work, sometimes about Jim's medication or about one of the children, until I learned to recognize them by a quality of loving urgency very unlike my ordinary thinking process.

This idea in my head now—if it had been anything except "Go to McDonald's," I would have said this was one of those times. But that was too ridiculous!

Wasn't it?

Marie and Jason scrambled into their chairs, still in pajamas on this one morning of the week when we could loaf around the house. Well, we could go to the drive-through window . . .

"Get your bathrobes on," I told them. "We're going to bring breakfast home from McDonald's."

"Yay!" shouted four-year-old Jason. "Can we get French fries?"

But Marie, two years older, looked from the waiting food to me, her face as bewildered as I felt.

Not the drive-through. Go inside to eat.

"On second thought," I called as the kids headed for their rooms, "let's put our clothes on and eat there."

"Boy," I heard Marie tell her brother, "does Mommy ever change her mind."

Twenty minutes later I was steering through Tulsa's Saturday traffic, as baffled as ever as to why we were doing this, when Marie burst into tears. "McDonald's makes me think of Daddy," she sobbed.

Jason was too young to remember the days when Jim could still drive and used to take the two of them out. But he wasn't too young to understand sorrow. "Don't cry, Marie," he said.

"Why don't we pray about it?" I interrupted. So we did, and then Marie said, "God's going to give us a new daddy."

"And someone who loves God," added Jason.

I said nothing. Not out loud. But inwardly I was crying, *No!* No one could replace Jim. Not ever. It wasn't that I was mourning, exactly. I'd done that during the years of seizures and pain. Death had come as such a release for Jim that I'd had to release him too. It was just that I wasn't ready to open up again to that kind of total involvement.

Before he died, Jim had asked me to remarry. "You're young, Shirley. You have your whole life ahead of you. Promise me you'll find someone else—when I'm gone."

But I don't want "someone else"! I protested inwardly as I pulled into the crowded McDonald's lot.

As I'd feared, on a Saturday morning there were long lines at the counter. Thinking ruefully of the eggs congealing in the skillet at home, I inched forward while the kids raced around the playground outside. At last I carried our trays to a window table.

That's where we were sitting when they came in, a stocky curly-haired man with a round, pleasant face— probably in his early forties—and three children, ages maybe twelve to five. I recognized the father at once: Terry Law, director of a singing group I'd seen on Oral

Roberts's TV program. Certainly no one I knew person-
ally. And yet. . . the unmistakable "impression" came as
I watched the four of them get into line at the counter:

This is the reason you are here.

These four people! This particular group, of all the
parents and children jamming the restaurant at this
moment?

I went on eating, but the food stuck in my throat.
Two years' experience in trusting God was insisting,
Introduce yourself. When I looked up they were setting
their trays down at the very next table.

Lord, I objected silently, *he doesn't know me! I can't
just say, "Hello, I'm Shirley."*

Then I remembered that a girl I'd known when I
was growing up back in Portland, Oregon, had joined
Terry Law's music group, Living Sound, several years
ago. I could ask Mr. Law about Paula.

He seemed sort of startled to have me speak to him.
Paula had married a young man from Living Sound, he
said, and together they were pastoring a church in
Alaska. He was still looking at me oddly. Probably wondering why I was butting in on the one day he had with
his family. More details about his work were coming
back to me. Living Sound traveled all over the world,
especially behind the Iron Curtain, where young people
turned out by the thousands to hear contemporary
music with a Christian message. He must hate to have

strangers break into his precious time at home.

Just being polite, no doubt, he asked some questions too. When I'd come to Tulsa from Portland, what the kids' names were, what my husband did.

"Jim died last spring," I said. "I'm a widow." Mr. Law set down his coffee container so hard it slopped over. He mopped it up quickly, said he was sorry about Jim, and wrote down my phone number to give to a lawyer he thought could be helpful. Then with an apology he turned back to the youngsters who were clamoring for his attention. *What in the world*, I wondered as Marie and Jason and I went out to our car, *had flustered him so? And what, for that matter*, I thought as I cleared away the cold remains of our uneaten breakfast back at home, *had this whole strange episode of dashing out to McDonald's been all about?*

I wasn't really expecting God to tell me. I'd learned to trust Him these past two years, not to understand Him. The trusting is everything: it's peace and joy and security long before the answers come. We see only a step at a time, so He can't usually tell us why.

Except that, in this case, He did . . .

Terry's story:

The conversation with Don Moen occurred on a Monday. Don was music director of our organization, Living Sound, and as usual he and I were aboard an airplane. This particular September day in 1984 we were returning from Arizona to our base in Tulsa, Oklahoma.

Our "base"—that's how I thought of Tulsa now: the place we traveled from. Not "home," not since my wife, Jan, died, even though our three beautiful kids were there, and my mother, who'd come down from Canada to care for Misty and Scot and Rebecca.

Across the aisle of the airplane, Don was watching me. "It's two years this month, Terry," he said, as though reading my thoughts.

Two years since my world had changed in as long as it takes for a car to leave the road and crash into a ditch. I'd been far away in England when it happened. No one ever knew what caused the accident. Perhaps the afternoon sun was directly in Jan's eyes on that east-west Oklahoma road.

I only knew that my life seemed to have ended along with hers. I plunged into a bottomless despair, unable to pray or work or believe that I would ever do these things again.

It was in this mood that I went to see my friend and mentor, Oral Roberts. Three months before I lost Jan, Oral had lost a son. "How do you keep going?" I asked him.

"I do it," he said, "by praising God."

Praise? When everything in me wanted to cry and curse? "I didn't say feel it," Oral said. "It is simply a fact that God is very great. Tell Him so."

As Oral predicted, praise was the road back into life. Hollow and mechanical at first, it soon became genuine. Praise for Jan. For the thirteen years we'd had together. For her faith. For knowing for sure that she was right now with Jesus.

Week by week the praise grew stronger—and so did my ability to do the things which at first had seemed impossible: to make plans, to travel, to minister to others around the world. Only the loneliness did not change. Praise helped me to live with the emptiness; it did not fill it.

Friends asked, of course, if I would consider marrying again. I knew I should, for the kids' sake. Eleven, nine, and four—how much they needed a mother!

I knew I should consider it for my mom's sake too. No one could have stepped in more selflessly than she had. But she'd raised her family. In justice she should be taking it easy now.

And yet . . . to consider marrying was just what I could not do. Every time I took my loneliness to God, He seemed to tell me: two years. It was always the same. I was not even to let the subject enter my head before that time. And that's what I'd told these friends.

Don was leaning across the narrow airplane aisle. "Two years," he repeated. "Remember what you said?"

"That I couldn't think about marrying for two years," I said. "And I haven't."

"Well, two years are up," Don persisted. "You'd better start thinking."

I leaned my head back in the seat, turning over my not-very-hopeful position. To me my three children were the greatest in the world, but what woman would want to take on marriage and motherhood all at once?

Where, for that matter, would I even meet an unmarried woman my own age? There were plenty of single girls in Living Sound, but they were kids in their twenties. I was forty-one. I'd want someone I could talk to. Someone who could understand the trauma that Misty and Scot and Rebecca had gone through.

I kept waiting for Don to pick up a magazine or something, but from the other side of the aisle he was regarding me expectantly.

"She'd have to be a widow," I heard myself say. "Someone who had as good a marriage as Jan and I had, and knows what it is to lose the most important person in your life. Anyhow," I finished, embarrassed at this outburst, "I don't know any widows."

"God does," Don said, "Let's pray about it."

"I will," I promised him, trying to close off a subject I wasn't ready for.

But Don had bowed his head. "Father, You know Terry's need, and his children's need. We believe You have a plan already at work . . ."

I glanced self-consciously at the other passengers. "Father," I joined in, keeping my voice as low as I could, "there's a widow somewhere who—"

"There's a widow in Tulsa," Don corrected.

"All right. In Tulsa. I ask that in Your own time—"

"Quickly."

"Okay. I ask that You quickly reveal . . ."

We prayed for several minutes, there on opposite sides of the aisle, I in generalities, Don in specifics. At the close, he stuck out his hand. With another nervous glance around, I reached across and gripped it.

"Thank You, Father," he pronounced, "that it's done."

Just like that. Prayer, in Don's view, didn't have to be long and eloquent. Just concrete and totally trusting.

At the office in Tulsa a number of crises were waiting for us. Living Sound had teams on the road both in the United States and Europe, including several Iron Curtain countries, and the week was hectic.

Crises or no, however, Saturdays belonged to the family. This was the morning, when I was in town, that I took the kids out to breakfast. And the outing always started with a debate.

"Grandy's," I suggested as we piled into the car, naming the place that made the pancakes I liked.

"Denny's," thirteen-year-old Misty voted.

"McDonald's," said six-year-old Rebecca.

"You just like the slide," Scot scoffed with the sophistication of one who has just turned eleven. "I say Denny's."

"Denny's wins!" cried Misty.

"Now wait a minute, you two," I said. "Rebecca hasn't gotten to choose for weeks. Let's let her decide today."

And that was how, a few minutes later, the four of us were standing in the line at the McDonald's counter, and I was gazing across the room at one of the most beautiful women I'd ever seen. Not a brunette beauty like Jan. This girl had hair the color of sunlight. In fact, where she sat at the window with two little tow-headed kids, the sun streaming through her long blond curls seemed to light up the room.

Maybe it was because I hadn't thought about marriage at all for two years, but l felt a stab of envy for her husband. I was thinking that it would be great just to sit near someone that pretty when, as we left the counter with our trays, the table next to her opened up.

I was trying to decide how to strike up a conversation when, to my surprise, she did it for me: "Aren't you Terry Law?" A friend of hers, it turned out, had sung for a while with Living Sound. We talked about her friend and then about anything I could think of. I found out that her kids were named Marie and Jason. Their mother's voice was as nice to listen to as her face was to look at.

I peeled the lid from my coffee container as I thought of more questions, like, "What does your husband do?"

When the girl with golden hair said, "I'm a widow,"

I took a swallow that scalded my throat all the way down.

What else I said to her I can't remember, except that I managed to get her phone number with some excuse about a lawyer. All l could hear was Don Moen's prayer on the airplane only five days earlier.

All I could think was, *Oh, Lord my God, You are very great!*

Editor's Note: Shirley and Terry were married in January 1985, five months after the "chance" meeting at McDonald's. A sixth child, Laurie Ann Law, was born in March 1986, "but she's not 'ours' any more than all the rest."

Our Bond

DIANE SCOTT AND JOHN BROCKINGTON

Diane: I'll never forget that night. I was twenty-two years old. It was a Monday night football game in 1971, a match-up between my team, the Green Bay Packers, and the Detroit Lions. A typical November night in Wisconsin—cold, wet, and miserable. Still, it was a full house at Milwaukee County Stadium.

I hunched in the stands wearing a Hefty bag to keep out the rain. Players slogged through the mud—slipping, getting nowhere, almost looking like they were in slow motion. Except one. Number 42, John Brockington. The Packers' running back. A rookie, but play after play, the ball went to him. He plowed through the line, outmaneuvered the defensive back, charged for the end zone, and brought the crowd to its feet.

I'd been a football fan my whole life, but I'd never seen a player like John. From that day on, he was my favorite. I knew one thing about this player. He had heart.

John: It was a big game for me. The first Monday night game of the year, and it put me on track for a 1,000-

yard season. I was blessed just to be carrying the ball in the NFL. I had no idea the real blessing of that night would come later.

Diane: Flash forward fifteen years. I moved to San Diego with my twins, Jessica and Justine. I'd gotten a great job teaching English at the University of California, San Diego. A couple of days a week I'd have lunch at a deli in Little Italy with a back garden, where I could sit in the sun with coffee and a stack of papers. The owner and I got to be friends. One day he noticed my Packers key chain.

"There's an ex-Packer who comes in here: John Brockington. He lives in the neighborhood. Ever hear of him?"

John: One day I stopped in at my local deli for a sandwich.

"I've got someone you should meet," the owner told me. "This is Diane. She's a big fan."

I shook hands with a pretty lady about half my size. Then we started talking football. She sure knew her stuff, especially about the Packers.

"I hope I see you around," she said.

"Me too," I told her.

Diane: John was one of the toughest NFL backs I'd ever seen, but in person he was incredibly gentle. Not soft, but kind. Spiritual. He put me at ease. Our conversations got a little longer, a little deeper. What do a college English professor and a retired NFL running back have to talk about? Lots, actually. Football, of course. But also faith, family. What's funny, important, interesting in life. John had gone through a divorce too. Soon we were going out to movies, football games, dinner. I introduced him to my girls, and they liked him right away. What would we be to each other—just good friends? One thing that hadn't changed about John since his playing days—he still had heart. And that still got to me.

John: Diane and I were on and off for years. Maybe it was because we'd both had marriages fall apart, but we were more than a little hesitant to commit.

It was during one of these separations that I first got sick, in June 2000. A slight pain in my side that wouldn't go away. Then I couldn't keep food down. My ankles swelled. It takes a lot to get me to the doctor. In this case, the intervention of my church friends, in particular Deborah, who's extra persistent.

The doctor ordered some tests. I went straight home afterward and conked out. The phone woke me up.

"Mr. Brockington," my doctor said, "the toxin level in your blood is lethally high. Get to the emergency room. Now."

Diane: I came home and found a message on my answering machine from a mutual friend. John was in intensive care. I didn't think twice about it. I went straight to the hospital. He looked awful. His lips were dry and cracked, his eyes yellow. He barely had the strength to squeeze my hand.

"Neither of John's kidneys are functioning," the doctor said. Basically his blood was being polluted. A healthy person's creatinine level—an indicator of kidney function—is around 1. At 7 or 8, patients usually start dialysis. John's was 44.4.

The doctor looked at John. "It's a miracle you're alive."

John: None of the doctors—not even my nephrologist, Dr. Fadda—could explain why I hadn't died. A lot of factors, they guessed. I had stayed in shape. I did not drink or smoke. Me, I credit God. The whole time I was in the ICU, I prayed. Giving thanks for the gifts God had blessed me with, the people he put in my life. Especially Diane. She never left my side. Every time I opened my eyes, there was Diane. Every time I thanked God.

Diane: John's illness stirred up my feelings for him. The same strong feeling I'd always had deep down inside: that somehow, we were connected in a way neither one of us should resist. Not now.

John: By monitoring my health and taking medication, I was able to stave off the inevitable: a transplant. In September 2001 Diane and I flew to Columbus, Ohio, where I was inducted into the hall of fame at my alma mater, Ohio State. But by the time we got back to San Diego, my creatinine level was through the roof.

"You'll have to start dialysis immediately," Dr. Fadda said.

It was tough being hooked up to that machine—four hours, three times a week. And it was no cure. I didn't want a transplant, but I couldn't delay it any longer.

Lord, is this Your plan for me?

"If you don't know a willing donor who matches, there's a four- to five-year wait for a kidney."

Dr. Fadda might as well have said it was all over. Who could I ask to make that kind of sacrifice? I thought about my family, my friends, my old teammates.

"Test me," Diane said.

Diane: Dr. Fadda explained that, ideally, an organ donor should be a close physical and genetic match with the recipient—usually a member of the same family. John's black. I'm white. He's 6 feet 1 and 240 pounds. I am 5 feet 2, 128 pounds.

"There's only the slimmest chance that you'd be suitable," the doctor said gently. "It's probably not even worth doing the tests."

John seemed relieved, but I just couldn't take no for an answer.

"Test me anyway," I insisted.

John: I didn't want Diane to go through with it. What if something went wrong? I would never forgive myself.

"Wait and see who else steps up," I pleaded. And in the following days, a lot of people did. Old teammates, college buddies, members of my church.

"It should be me," Diane insisted. The chances were overwhelming Diane would not be a match.

Diane: How's this for an answer to prayer? I was a good match.

"I still can't advise it," the doctor said. "You're so much smaller. Your kidney won't be big enough to sustain him."

I asked him to do a sonogram. He could not believe the results. "You have the biggest kidneys I've ever seen in a woman your size!"

Not your average compliment, but I was sure glad to hear it.

John: The operation was a success, with Diane's kidney doing its job right away.

Afterward my doctor told me, "You have no idea what the odds were against this."

But I did. And I knew it was more than just a statistical long shot. Diane and I were brought together for a reason, a reason we struggled to accept. In the end it was made clear. We were a good match.

Diane: John and I went back to work on our relationship. You'd think it would have been easy after the transplant, right? I guess love is never easy, never uncomplicated, not when it comes to giving all of yourself to another. Maybe that's why it took us ten years of testing each other—testing our love and commitment—until John and I became husband and wife.

Of course, there has always been that one thing about John, ever since that cold, rainy night in Milwaukee. He had so much heart. And now he has mine.

CHAPTER 2

Love's Greatest Treasure

Where your treasure is, there your heart will be also.
(Matthew 6:21, NIV)

We often spend our lives thrashing about in the world looking for some kind of special treasure—money, romance, fame. We tend to look in all the wrong places for those pseudotreasures, and we are bitterly disappointed. At long last, we wander dejectedly back home to the place where we know we are accepted and loved, no matter what. We come home to our family. And there we find what has been waiting for us all along . . . love's greatest treasure.

The Nightlight

NANCY JO ECKERSON

As a child, I was in awe of Mother. She was tall, thin, and as graceful as a swaying willow tree. At a very young age she had suffered from polio so severe that it stunted the growth of her left hip. But not even polio could deter this amazing woman from projecting an image of pure poise. She forced herself to practice walking until she showed such style that at twenty years old, she was hired as a model for Filene's and Jordan Marsh of Boston.

She was blessed with many talents. After marriage she used her musical talents to enrich the life of two churches in the center of our village. Mother's talent as an organist and choir director brought the congregations much joy. She had the voice of an angel. Her delicate soprano tone glided easily from deep inside her soul. I remember accompanying her to church on Thursday afternoons. I would bring my homework and sit in one of the pews while she practiced the next Sunday's hymns. Occasionally Mother would whisper to me, "Come and sing with me, Nancy."

I would eagerly jump up and scoot in alongside of her. "I love singing with you, Momma." My deep alto voice boomed through the church. Little did I know that I was absorbing the sounds that would sustain me throughout my life.

At home I made up silly parodies of these great hymns. "Amazing Grace" lent itself to amazing fun. "Amazing Grace, how swift the sound, that caught a wretch like me. I once was lost, but soon Mom found . . . me in the maple tree." Mother feigned disapproval of my creations, but I know I would sometimes catch her holding back a smile.

Despite her schedule of providing music for two churches, Mother always prepared a delicious Sunday dinner. My favorite was roast beef with Yorkshire pudding. Not a Sunday passed that we didn't have a spectacular dessert, like chocolate soufflé or Boston crème pie. "If you children eat all your vegetables, I have a special dessert for you." There was no argument from my brothers or me; we knew it would be delicious and well worth the agony of some peas or squash.

Mother's manners and speech were impeccable. She was raised the youngest daughter of a well-respected bank president in New England. Her mother was a petite, charming lady from Sweden. I, on the other hand, was raised in a farm village with mostly boys for neighbors. I was tiny and tough with a real penchant for tree climbing and bike wars. I would hear the boys shout, "Ditch her," and in a matter of seconds I would be thrown from my bike. "I'll get you for that," came my screams! A true tomboy, I always wore two or three bandages like badges of honor.

My childhood hero was Annie Oakley. For years I dressed in Annie Oakley outfits, arguing when I wasn't allowed to bring my gun to the dinner table, "Mom! I have to have the gun . . . what if JD or Steve tries to rob us?"

"Nancy, that gun is not something a lady brings to the table. You will have to leave it in the other room. Don't worry, your father will keep your brothers in line." Perhaps she was somewhat understanding of the dilemma with the boys, but still she took away my gun. Years later, unbeknownst to Mother, I won awards for my skill on the rifle range at the YMCA camp.

Occasionally, I would dress up for dinner in my Sunday best. Mother would call us inside. "Coming, Mom," I'd yell from the top of the cherry tree. Slithering down the trunk, my gaze met Mom scowling. "Oh, Nancy, look at your outfit," she would just sigh. Once, I came to the dinner table covered with hives from snitching berries out of Mom's strawberry patch. Mom looked at me as if to say, "My poor, pathetic, splotchy child!" At times like these I felt she loved me as you love a stray cat. It was more a charitable act than anything else.

She was not outwardly affectionate, and I was a hop-on-your-lap-and-kiss-you kind of kid. We were as different as night and day. She must have been so disappointed in this alien creature she had given birth to.

As time passed and I had children of my own, I gained a great deal of wisdom. I began to realize that my mom had done a lot for my brothers and me. More than likely, she had known a lot too. That epiphany came to me when I went to pick up my daughter from church camp. The list of her activities was plain to see. I thought about my sneaky riflery stunt—maybe I hadn't been the sneaky one, after all?

One particular year, I remember Christmas shopping for a toy for my daughter. She, and every other little girl, had asked Santa for a Cabbage Patch doll. It was a fad that caught on like wildfire; so there wasn't one to be found. I thought of giving up the search until I remembered a special Christmas in my childhood. "Mom, please, I have to have that jacket. It's so pretty and everyone at school has a ski jacket. It's reversible, Mom, I can wear it all the time and I'll take really good care of it!" I already had a winter jacket from the previous year that still fit. I certainly didn't need this one.

Christmas morning arrived, and after all the gifts were opened my Mother came into the living room with one more package. She handed it to me with a smile. As I opened it I shrieked, "Oh, Mom! This is the best Christmas ever!" She really understood the importance for a brand-new teenager to feel a part of the "in" crowd.

Following my mother's generous example, I persisted in my search for the Cabbage Patch doll for my daughter.

Her joy on Christmas morning brought back thoughts of my own happiness on that day so long ago.

Mother graduated summa cum laude from Cornell University and later returned to college in 1970 for her master's degree. She graduated in 1972 with a degree in library science.

For those two years Mom and I attended college simultaneously. I would call her to complain about the workload. "Mom! That professor is insane! He thinks we can write a ten-page paper and read seven chapters in the text all by Monday!"

"The man is nuts, sweetie. Maybe you can call the white coats from next door and have him committed!" Mom laughed. She knew just what to say to release the tension and make me laugh too.

It was her turn to call, "Nancy, I am so discouraged. I spent a week writing this paper, researching, documenting and rewriting. The professor gave me a B–! I can't believe it."

"Mom, if you really feel you deserve more, why not make an appointment to meet with him and point out why you think so."

A week later, "Nancy, you were a lifesaver. I met with the professor and he agreed. My grade was changed to an A-. Thank you for the advice." I was bowled over by the thought that I could give her encouragement.

We bonded in such a way that I began to feel valued

and worthy more than ever. It was the best time of our whole lives together. Finally, life was sweet.

But those years came to an abrupt end when a beastly disease tore them from us! Every time I phoned her, she was more withdrawn and seemed anxious to get off the phone. We were drifting apart, and my heart just ached. But not knowing that Alzheimer's disease was ravaging her body, every slip of mind she suffered pushed my newfound feeling of security away. I was sure I had caused this rift between us. Once again, I couldn't do anything right, I thought.

With the perfect vision that only hindsight affords, I now realize that she was cognizant of the changes in her capabilities and was making Herculean efforts to preserve her dignity by purposefully keeping our conversations short. She was losing her ability to communicate at only forty-nine years old.

When she was admitted to a nursing home at fifty-seven years old, my world fell apart. I had my first experience with panic attacks. Watching her deteriorate was catastrophic to me. The day she no longer recognized my children or me was the worst day of my life.

When my children were eight and ten years old, Mom lost her battle with Alzheimer's. I was thirty-six and shattered. I went to check on my kids that night. I knew they had heard me crying; I wanted them to see that I was still there for them. As I entered my son's room, he said, "Mommy, Nana is fine. She said to tell you." Dazed, not knowing how to respond, I held him tight. A sense of peace came to me then, and I felt closer to her once more.

Eleven years later, I faced yet another trauma. My husband and I were having serious marital troubles that led to separation. One month later, my routine chest x-ray showed streaks from my cigarette smoking. I had to quit my three-packs-a-day habit immediately. With these two heartbreaks, I was in crisis once more. The tough little tomboy had fallen apart from life's tragedies. I remember crying, "Mom, I wish you could come down here and hug me and make things all better."

The first night that I was alone after twenty-five years of marriage I plodded into my bedroom and crawled onto my bed. A flood of tears let loose, and I sobbed. Just then the nightlight by my bed began blinking on and off. I was amazed, as that very nightlight had ceased to work long ago. My tears disappeared as I kept my eye on the light, and my fears began to subside. Eventually, I drifted off to sleep. When I awoke, the mysterious nightlight had quit working again. This became the pattern every night. I would no sooner get into my bed than the light would start blinking.

One night, I didn't think I could go on. The divorce papers were now signed, and I was in agony from nicotine withdrawal. I fell to my knees by the tiny nightlight.

It blinked wildly! I looked more closely at the picture. It was a beautiful maternal looking angel holding a precious, childlike angel. They looked like Mom and me. Even their hair color was the same as ours. I was in awe! I knew in my heart that I would get through all this. I also knew that the nightlight was my mother's connection with me.

Months later, I moved out of my family home of twelve years. I left many things behind, but I unplugged my angel nightlight and brought it with me. What if it doesn't ever light up again? What if it was a short in the wiring all this time? The first night, all alone in my new place, I was very nervous. I walked into the bedroom and found the nightlight blinking uncontrollably. *Oh, Mom! You are here with me.*

Throughout my childhood I saw only the differences between my mother and me. I felt that I could never bridge the gap and feel close to someone so perfect. I was a goofy girl, and she was a lovely lady.

It was nothing short of miraculous. From beyond the grave, Mom found a way to reach me and give me strength. I now know she loves me. I'm certain she always did.

A Sign

DENNIS THOMSON AS TOLD TO
PATTI MAGUIRE ARMSTRONG

Nothing in my thirty-nine years as a Boston police officer had prepared me for the news that my twenty-
year-old son, Dennis, had been in a serious car accident.
He was in training with the U.S. Air Force in Florida, but
had taken a long weekend to visit friends in Mississippi.

It was one of his friends that called my wife,
Maureen, while I was at work, to tell us that a drunken
driver had collided head-on with Dennis. No one knew
his condition, and the hospital would not release that
information over the phone. Within a couple of hours I
was on a flight to Mississippi. Maureen stayed with our
other two children, Danielle, who was eighteen at the
time, and David, fourteen.

I never felt so alone as I did on that plane ride.
Gripped by fear of the unknown, I was not a part of the
world around me. There was no one to cry out to; no
one to help me except for God. "Lord, please let Dennis
be all right," I prayed unceasingly.

At the hospital, I learned that Dennis was in a coma.

I desperately yearned to hear the doctor console me with news that everything would be okay. Instead, he would not venture a prognosis other than to say there were three possibilities. Dennis could come out of the coma and be fine, he could come out of it and suffer brain damage, or he could die. I latched on to the first possibility. "Dear God, please save my boy," I prayed as we walked to his room.

Seeing my dear son surrounded by machines and tubes, love and fear washed over me. I had been to many accidents with the police department. I thought I had seen it all, but this was my son. "Dennis, I'm here," I whispered. "I love you." I prayed quietly at his bedside for about twenty minutes. Then, overwhelmed with emotion, I went down to the hospital chapel.

On my knees, before God, I broke down for the first time. Tears and anger gushed forth. "Lord, why are You punishing me? What have I done?" I cried out. "You could have stopped this! Why didn't You save my son?"

But as I emptied myself of emotions, I was finally left with just my faith. I believed that God had a plan for everyone. This was part of His plan. "Lord, if it is Your will, please save my son," I prayed.

I returned to Dennis's room. Looking at his bruised and swollen face, I pleaded with God not to take him. He had been a part of me since the day he was born.

From the moment Dennis entered the world, it became

a brighter place for me. Never had I experienced such happiness as I did looking into his perfect little newborn face. As a cop, I was a tough guy. But holding the miracle of my baby boy, I experienced love as never before. Life would never be the same.

Although Dennis had been given my same name, he was not just a "chip off the old block." He was different. My son David is probably more like me; we tend to keep our emotions to ourselves. But Dennis was demonstrative and free with his feelings. He loved everyone and was not afraid to show it. In turn, it seemed everyone loved him.

One of his earliest loves was baseball. It was a love affair that began at five years old during his first Little League season. Dennis was an all-around athlete, but baseball was his true love. One of my proudest moments was watching Dennis at the age of fifteen, smack a major-league home run out of the field. I frequently made deals with guys at work, promising to cover for them if they would work for me so I would not miss his games.

Other kids looked up to Dennis. He was a natural leader and was elected vice president in high school. Besides sports, Dennis was an altar boy who served with enthusiasm. It was his own idea one year to volunteer to serve Midnight Christmas Mass. Naturally, the rest of the family decided to be there with him too. We all looked to Dennis. He was a loving son and big brother his younger siblings adored.

Dennis entered college and was selected as a starting player on the baseball team. But books and classrooms encumbered his exuberant personality. He craved hands-on learning and experiences. So, he joined the U.S. Air Force in 2003 and loved it.

The next day, Maureen arrived. Relatives had offered to stay with the other children. I held her hand tightly as we walked to Dennis's room. No words were necessary or adequate. Our pain was indescribable, and the only comfort was in knowing we shared it with each other.

Maureen never left our son's side except to sleep and eat. However, I could only stay for short visits, coming and going throughout the day. Seeing Dennis so helpless, overwhelmed me with a feeling of uselessness. I had always been there for him when he was growing up. There was nothing I would not have done for him, but now there was nothing I could do but pray.

After ten days, I felt the need to return to our younger two children. They were grieving too. Maureen could stay with Dennis, and I would get back to work and try to put a routine back into our home. I went to his room one last time. "Good-bye, Dennis," I said, choking back the tears. "I love you." My heart ached. Would we ever see each other again?

At home, the kids and I just went through the motions of our day. School for them and work for me. And always prayer. Maureen called daily. There was never any sign of improvement. Not quite two weeks after I returned home, the phone rang at 4 a.m. Even before I answered, I knew Dennis would not be coming home. I woke the kids up. Danielle cried, but it would take David another week to do so. He was so much like me. Life would go on. We would go on. But we knew it would never be the same. A part of us was gone.

Maureen and I knew Dennis was loved by many, but we were overwhelmed to learn just how many. Lines snaked outside the funeral parlor. The funeral Mass was "standing room only." For many weeks afterward, we still received letters from teachers, students, parents, friends . . . it seemed everywhere he went, Dennis had touched people.

But as life once again became routine, I struggled to go on. Would the sun ever shine again? Would my heart ever stop hurting?

"God," I prayed one day in anguish. "I know Dennis is with you, but can you send me a sign to let me know he's all right?" I was hoping for some sort of comfort and connection with my son.

A few days later, Maureen and I were having dinner at a restaurant. Danielle called us on our cell phone. The father of Dennis's friend, Joseph "Fitzy" Fitzpatrick, had called our house to tell us he discovered a new billboard hanging over Fenway Park with our son in the picture.

It was late, so Maureen and I returned home that

evening. But the first thing in the morning we headed to Fenway Park. Bigger than life, "Fitzy" was pictured clenching the home-run ball he had just caught. His buddy, our son Dennis, is on the right, smiling wide under his Red Sox cap. Another buddy, Neil Gavin, is at his side cheering.

Encountering our son's happy face over the stadium, we cried tears of both grief and joy. That was our boy—our baseball-loving boy—smiling down at us. Our tears soon turned to laughter. Leave it to Dennis to pull off something like this.

Dennis had loved baseball. He was in his element, at a baseball game surrounded by friends. The picture in the billboard was over the ticket booth advertising ticket sales. It was taken two years before he died. Of all the thousands of pictures that could have been used, it was the one with my son that ended up on the billboard. It had to be an answer to my prayer. I had received my sign—literally.

From that day forth, I began to breathe easier, and I experienced peace. I'm okay now, and I know my son is too.

A Rose in the Snow

FLORENCE DELANEY

By the time I was twelve years old I had been a winner three years in a row in the Davis Park races that were part of the July Fourth celebrations in my hometown of Scarsdale. I was a cheerleader for my grammar school football team, and my speciality was doing cartwheels at halftime. And when I wasn't in school, dungarees and sneakers were what I wore, since they were the best for climbing trees.

But then I was stricken with polio. By the age of fourteen, my legs were in braces. I was on crutches and realized I had to give up forever all those activities I loved so much. It was hard for me to accept.

When December came, and the air was cold and the winter trees showed their bony limbs, I felt as far from God as I had ever been.

Then I heard that a Paulist priest, Father Sullivan, was coming to our parish to lead a novena—nine days of services and prayers—devoted to Our Lady of Guadalupe.

I had always loved the story of the miracle of Guadalupe. In 1531 Juan Diego, a poor Mexican Indian who had recently lost his beloved wife, was full of doubt about the goodness of God, for he felt that God was remote from his tragic loss. But on a cold December morning Our Lady of Guadalupe appeared and assured Juan that he was precious to God. And as a sign of that love there grew, among the barren rocks in the chilling wind, clusters of glorious Castilian roses.

Like Juan I, too, felt that God was detached from my suffering. So when I heard about this novena, I eagerly decided to attend.

I thought I might receive a sign that God had not forgotten me either.

On the first night of services, my mother helped me bundle up, and when my father came home from work, he drove me to the church and sat beside me in the front pew. Father Sullivan told us that on the last of the nine nights of services, everyone who had attended faithfully would receive a red rose.

I was excited. I wanted the rose. I wanted a sign that I was loved.

Night after night, every night, my father or mother drove me to church and sat with me in the pew for the hourlong service. Many nights, at the end of the day when I was tired and my legs ached, I didn't feel like going out in the cold, but I knew I had to push myself. I wanted that rose.

Finally it was the last day of the novena. And all day long we had a terrible snowstorm.

I sat at the window for hours, watching for the snowplow to come and clear our street. I tried to do my homework to keep busy, but my thoughts were really on the snow that might end up keeping me at home.

Late in the afternoon the snowplow came, and I called my father at his office in New York City.

"Tonight's the night I get my rose, Dad!" I told him excitedly. "When will you be home?"

He came in late, after waiting a long time for his train, and stomped the snow from his boots. "You look exhausted," my mother said to him.

"I'm worried about Florence," my father said. "Do you think she should go out in this weather?" I held my breath in panic. I had to go tonight.

I sat nervously through dinner listening to the wind howling in the blackness outside. At times it sounded as though tree limbs were coming down. The rest of the family seemed to be savoring the warmth and shelter of the indoors. But all I could think about was going out— to get my rose.

At last my father put down his fork and pushed back his chair. "I'll take you to church now, Florence," he said.

My brother Jimmie stood up. "You won't be able to get the car out of the driveway, Dad," he said. "I'd better shovel you out." He pulled on his heavy jacket, opened the door, and stepped back. "This wind is mean," he said.

My brother Johnnie got up too. "I'll come out and help you," he said.

I walked slowly to the car, clinging to my father's arm with my right hand while holding my crutch with my left. At the end of the icy walk, my mother ran after us holding out my mittens. "You forgot these!" she said, pulling them on with a little pat. "If your hands are warm, your whole body will feel warm."

Dad and I drove through the quiet neighborhood. No one else was out because of the storm, but even in the bitter cold, I smiled because I knew what was waiting for me.

As we drove into the parking lot of the church, I saw that it hadn't been plowed.

"It'll be hard going to get you through that, Florence," my father said. "But we'll do it." When we got out of the car, he walked just ahead of me, breaking the force of the bitter wind and stomping down the snow with his galoshes. I held tightly to his outstretched hand as he struggled to keep me up and help me along. The moon was shrouded with mist, and it shed an icy light as I pulled myself along in my father's footsteps. "Dad," I said, shouting into the icy wind, "I don't think I can make it."

"You can make it, Florence."

I pulled the wool collar of my jacket up high and pulled in my head like a turtle, hoping my father wouldn't see the tears running down my cheeks; they were the only things that felt warm.

Inside, the church was warm and quiet. Still shivering from the cold, we sat in the front pew. There were only four other worshipers there.

Father Sullivan came over to greet us with a big smile. He shook my father's hand, and I took my mittens off so he could shake mine.

"I'm really surprised to see you out on a night like this," he said. And then he hesitated, as though reading my mind. "It's such a dreadful night . . . I hate to tell you this—the florist wasn't able to come."

"Do you mean I won't get my rose?" I asked. My voice was so low I could hardly hear it.

"I'm truly sorry," he said. "I hope you're not too disappointed."

I nodded weakly and tried to smile. I knew it wasn't Father Sullivan's fault. He couldn't control the weather. "It's okay," I heard myself saying. But I really felt like crying.

By the time the service was over, the wind had died down. I stumbled along through the parking lot, trying to make sense out of what had happened.

"Dad," I said in the car on the way home, "why didn't I get my rose?"

"I don't know, Florence," he said. He reached over and put his big hand over my mittened ones. The hands in which I'd thought I'd carry home a rose . . . a sign from God that I was loved.

I pressed my mittens against my face, trying not to cry. My mittens. My mother had rushed out in the bitter cold to put them on my hands so I'd be warm.

I sat absolutely still as the car pulled into the driveway—the driveway that my brothers had come out on an icy night to shovel.

My father opened the car door to help me out, and I reached for his arm—the arm that had guided me and supported me all evening long.

I had received a sign.

A sign from God that I was loved.

A Half Hour Early

ELIZABETH BLAKE

My elderly mother sat on the living room couch watching TV as I plumped the pillows behind her. "I'm going outside now to read," I told her. "I'll come back inside in half an hour. Alani's coming over later to visit."

"Good. I'll sit and watch *Wheel of Fortune*," she said. Her skill at solving word puzzles exceeded mine, and I knew she'd be entertained while I took a break.

A few months before, she had fallen and broken her neck. Although this terrible accident traumatized our family, we knew God had protected her. The doctors said, "It's a miracle she isn't paralyzed. She'll have to wear a neck brace for a while."

After four months of recovering in a nursing home, the brace came off and she moved in with me. Since she weighed 200 pounds and was weak, caring for her was difficult. I looked forward to her regaining strength.

Her care consumed my days from seven in the morning to eleven in the evening. I felt overwhelmed and alone, and I prayed for God's intervention for her quick recovery. I knew it would take another miracle.

At four o'clock every busy afternoon, I treated myself to one relaxing hour on my back patio, enjoying the beautiful Arizona weather. When the melody "Für Elise" floated throughout the house every day at 5:00 sharp, I knew it was time to go back indoors and start dinner. My trusty timer always kept me on schedule.

But this particular day was different. I had to go back inside at 4:30 to start dinner *a half hour early*, because my four-year-old granddaughter was coming over later to visit.

"Your blood sugar has been good lately," I told Mother. "You'll be fine." She smiled and nodded her understanding. Breaking her neck had shocked my mother's system, and her blood sugar had shot up to 200, but with medication we had gotten it back down to a normal 100. After two months of constantly checking her blood sugar, I was finally able to relax my constant vigil.

As usual, I went out to the back patio. Sunlight warmed my face, giving me a feeling of peace and comfort. Birds chirped melodic songs and tall trees swayed in the gentle breeze. My lungs took in a deep breath of clean air, and I thanked God for the beauty He had given us. Somehow I sensed God's peaceful presence, and my lips formed a tired smile. Thirty minutes went by quickly, especially since I was used to a full hour's rest.

At 4:30 I came indoors early to prepare dinner. As I passed my mother on the couch, I noticed she had a strange expression on her face. *That's odd. She looks confused.* I moved closer to her and tried to get her attention, but she simply sat there with a vacant smile, staring into space.

"Mother?" No response. "Do you know who I am?" A slight shake of the head.

I started pumping her with questions. "Do you know what year this is?" Then I began to shout. "Do you know your name?" Still no response.

Alarm bells clanging in my head, I rushed to the bedroom to get her glucometer. With trembling hands, I stuck her finger to test her blood sugar. It read a dangerously low 45!

Forcing myself not to panic, I ran to the kitchen. Tearing open the freezer door, I yanked out food until I found some frozen concentrate to make some juice. I tried giving her some, but it dribbled down her chin— she couldn't swallow it.

I then dialed 911.

It was just minutes, although it seemed like hours, before ambulance sirens blaring in the distance headed our way. Mother started to slump over while I frantically tried to hold on to her.

A fire engine pulled up in front, and paramedics rushed into the house. One took her blood pressure. Another asked me questions and filled out paperwork. Another tested her blood sugar. "Her sugar is *25!*" he shouted. Mother began slipping off the couch.

With authority, they immediately pulled out their IV

equipment, wrapped a tourniquet around her arm and searched for a vein, which is always difficult because she has terrible veins. Her eyes began to roll back into her head. *Please, God, help them find a vein.* Yes! They got it right away. I whispered a quick prayer of thanks.

Soon, they pushed the life-giving glucose into her IV.

For an eternal minute we waited, when suddenly she sat up and looked around, gazing in amazement at all the strangers watching her. One of the paramedics tested her blood sugar again. This time a smile crossed his face. "It's 200," he reported. They wanted it high, to give her system a boost, until she had time to recover.

Then there was lots of paperwork. "You'd better take her to the hospital," they advised me.

Of course, Mother didn't want to go. Looking around at all the people who surrounded her, she insisted, "I don't need to go to the hospital. I was just taking a nap."

We all looked at each other and laughed with relief at the humor of it. She hated hospitals, and I didn't want to subject her to more poking, prodding, and testing. I hoped it had only been a suggestion and not a requirement.

I asked them, "Is that really necessary?"

"Yes," they insisted.

A voice inside me whispered, *"Listen to the paramedics."* I took their advice and agreed to send her, against her protests.

The crew loaded her into the ambulance for transport to the hospital. They were gone in a flash. I rushed around the house grabbing medical records and some clothing for her, then phoned my daughter to tell her what had happened.

I started out the door for the hospital. As I turned to grab my purse, my hand froze as the melody of "Für Elise," my alarm, chimed throughout the house. My eyes darted to the kitchen clock—it read 5:00! I gulped as I realized this was the usual time for me to come back inside the house. *Thank you God for arranging my schedule so I had to come in a half hour early today.*

I jumped into my car and rushed to the hospital. The registration clerk in the emergency room asked me questions and made out a chart. It was 5:30 before I entered Mother's room. A small army of hospital personnel surrounded her while a nurse pushed something into the IV.

"What is that?" I asked.

"Glucose," the nurse said.

I couldn't believe it. My voice rose to a high pitch. What were they doing? "Why are you giving her glucose? Her glucose level is 200!"

"No it's not," the nurse said. "It's 45."

When I realized this, I gulped. Again I whispered a prayer. *Thank You, God, for that still, small voice persuading me to listen to the paramedics and send her to the hospital.* It scared me to think of what might have happened if I hadn't listened to them. I wouldn't have been able to handle her erratic blood sugar.

The E.R. doctor explained that she wasn't metabolizing her diabetes medication any longer. It took five days to stabilize her.

After I brought her home again, I had to test her sugar level four times a day. In time she improved and eventually stopped taking diabetes medication altogether, becoming stronger and healthier. Eventually she could get out of bed on her own, walk with a walker, and dress herself, becoming more independent. God had answered my prayers. My burden had been lifted, and it became a joy to care for her.

As I look back on that day, I realize that if I hadn't come indoors until 5:00, as was my routine, I would have found my mother unconscious on the couch or it might have been too late. A mere thirty minutes, that God arranged, made the difference between life and death. I don't feel alone or overwhelmed anymore. I know that God was watching over us that day, and today as well. I know now that I'm not my mother's only caregiver—I have the Lord helping me. We are never alone. And that's the best miracle.

The Christmas Gift
of Love

CHRISTINE TROLLINGER

Christmas of 2005 will always live in our hearts as an ending and a new beginning. My husband had battled cancer for most of his life. This last battle was not to be won.

Early in December my husband had called my name rather urgently from the chair in the living room where he now spent most of his time, tethered to oxygen and all the paraphernalia associated with illness. I was startled by the sound of urgency in his voice. I thought he must have been having another breathing crisis, as I quickly made my way from the kitchen to help him. Instead I discovered that he was struggling to find a pen and a paper to write out something he said was very important.

He had just come home from the hospital the day before, and the prognosis was not good. The cancer had spread to his lungs. I think he knew deep in his heart that he would not live through Christmas this year. He was trying to make sure we would all have a joyful Christmas no matter the outcome of this present crisis. As I watched my beloved struggle to write out his important list, my heart was breaking. I could see that each hour he was slipping further and further away from me.

When he finished, he was anxious to explain each item that he had written down. It was a list of gifts, which he wanted me to buy for our children for Christmas. He explained to me that he had decided early in July that he wanted this Christmas to be especially filled with laughter and with joy.

The secret to the gifts on his list was a memory of the prior July fourth celebration when we had all gathered at my daughter's new home in the country. They had just moved into their new country estate the previous month. Gene had teased Robin and Mike about their becoming just like the couple on the old TV series *Green Acres,* and he got a big smile as he recounted how funny it struck him when Robin was riding the tractor they had just purchased to keep the twenty-one acres mowed. He said she reminded him of Eva Gabor.

As he recounted the reason for her particular gift, his eyes shown with such love and joy that I could see by his expression he was imagining the giggles he hoped his gift would give her on Christmas Day. For

Robin, he had instructed that I buy her diamonds and overalls.

Then he pointed to the next gift on his list. Gene's note for Randy was a set of new tires. He smiled as I gave him a rather puzzled look to which he replied, "I know it sounds strange, but Randy's tires were looking mighty thin and dangerous on that day back in July." He smiled again and said, "Make sure Randy stays safe and has many good memories as he travels to our favorite fishing holes next summer."

The last item was for our younger son, Russ. His instructions were to buy him a painting of the Kansas City Chiefs' football team that would represent all the wonderful times they had enjoyed through the years. His eyes grew a bit tearful as he struggled to explain that he didn't think he would be able to attend any more Chiefs games with Russ, but he wanted Russ to know he would be there in spirit. Sports were a big part of their father-and-son relationship. The last game they had planned to attend together was the opening game for the Chiefs season. They had planned it that very fourth of July day.

As Gene handed me his precious gift list, I managed to swallow back the tears and assure him that I would make sure I bought each item on the list, and he could help me wrap them. Quietly he slipped further and further away in the next few days. Before I could accomplish his shopping, he returned to the hospital for the final time on December 9. My beloved husband lost his final battle with cancer just twelve days before Christmas on December 13.

After the funeral, I retrieved Gene's precious Christmas list from the note board in the kitchen, where I had put it for safekeeping the day he had given it to me. My heart felt much too heavy and my mind much too burdened with the pain of his loss to go out shopping, but I resolved that I would accomplish my mission somehow because it had meant so much to Gene.

Looking at the list, I suddenly realized that at least one item I had managed to buy without much effort. That gave me hope that I would somehow accomplish the shopping for the other two children.

The gift of new tires for our oldest was arranged the day of the funeral. Randy's car broke down, and he had to take my car to get home. I had already had his car towed to the shop for a new starter, which Randy had asked me to do. I had instructed them to install new tires while they were making Randy's requested repair.

As I set out to do the shopping, I had no idea how I would ever find the other items listed. Steeling myself to honor my beloved's last wishes, I walked into the mall feeling totally disoriented. As I began the trek through throngs of joyful shoppers, my heart felt like lead. But in an instant, all that would change.

At the first turn in the mall, there in the window of

a shop was the last item on the list. It was the one I felt I would never be able to find. Hanging there in plain sight was an artist's original painting of the Kansas City Chiefs. It was fabulously done and exactly as my husband had envisioned it to be in his little note.

The next problem was how to pay for such an item. I was certain it must be much too expensive for my strained budget. After enquiring about the price from the shop's owner, I was almost speechless that it was the exact amount Gene had budgeted for our son's gift. The next problem came when the credit card machine would not connect to the credit center. The lines were down, and she had no way to verify a purchase. The shop's owner was a bit frustrated, but she came up with a solution. A solution, which would prove heaven sent.

She instructed me to go to the mall's ATM machine and gave me directions to where it was located. I set out to get the cash and rush back to buy the painting. Hurrying as fast as I could to the other end of the mall, I retrieved the needed purchase price and turned to make the walk back to the shop. Just as I turned back into the corridor, there in a side hallway, was the second item on the list—a butterfly pendant and earrings my husband had instructed me to buy for our daughter, Robin.

I had made some calls to the local jewelry shops the day before to no avail. No one had carried such a special set as Gene had described. But against all odds, there it was. Gene loved the story of the butterfly and what it symbolizes to those who believe in eternal life. The butterfly symbolizes the resurrection of all men, derived from the three stages of butterfly's life: caterpillar, chrysalis, and butterfly—hence life, death, and resurrection. I felt Gene was trying to let our daughter know that he was still present at our celebration and that he would always watch over his little girl. The little diamond chips in the set were also absolutely perfect. I had already purchased the overalls at Wal-Mart.

With a much lighter heart, I found my way back to the shop where the painting was. It all came into place with those last two purchases. God was there with us all. He understood the grief we felt, but He wanted us to celebrate the greatest treasure of Christmas—the treasure of eternal life and the gift of His Son. It was a gift that would make it possible for our circle of love to remain unbroken and our spirits to rejoice even in the midst of sorrow.

If I Could Just Phone Home

ELIZABETH J. SCHMEIDLER

While saying my prayers one night just before 11:00, I was praying for comfort for the families of two relatively young men who had recently died. Both were dedicated physicians. Both were men of faith. As I pondered their passing, I was fervently wishing that I could somehow comfort their families, either by figuring out a good reason that God would have called them home, or by giving them a glimpse of God's promise of "No eye has seen, no ear has heard, what God has prepared for those who love him" (1 Corinthians 2:9, NIV).

Suddenly, I remembered the time when my oldest son, Jerome, was given the opportunity to go to Mexico for two weeks with one of our priests and several boys from our local Catholic high school. He was fifteen at the time, and I had never "let him out of my pocket" so to speak. I am a stay-at-home mom, and of course, very cautious where my kids are concerned. I've never been to another country, so needless to say, my view of Mexico was skewed by television . . . I was picturing banditos and constant drug busts and my son being unjustly arrested by the Mexican police. I know it sounds silly . . . it was, but it was hard to let go! I prayed for peace and for his safety and finally along with my husband, said yes.

It was a tearful day when he left. I repeatedly told God that I was sorry for crying over a "two week trip to Mexico," but I suppose there was more to my tears than just worry . . . I think it was the whole "he's growing up" thing. Anyway, I knew I was going to miss him.

The very next night after he left, the priest had all the boys phone home. I'll never forget that call. Jerome was so excited, he couldn't talk fast enough:

"Mom, you should see the *ocean*! It is so *beautiful* here! Mom, you should *taste* the food! We are living with this little Mexican woman who makes us *fresh* tortillas and real refried beans! Mom, you should see the all the flowers! You would love them! The weather is so perfect here! I am having so much fun!"

He went on and on and on. The joy in his voice alone was enough to put a stopper in my tear ducts! When I replaced the receiver I thought to myself, *How could I possibly be sad that he is gone when he is so happy?* It was at that very moment that a thought came to me: *It's too bad that our loved ones can't "phone home" from heaven. If they could just tell us how happy they are, then our pain would be greatly reduced.*

As I lay in bed remembering that specific memory, I realized that maybe I could write a song about "phoning home." Though it was late, I sprung out of bed and went to the computer. I knew from past experience that when God calls me to write something, it would come out very quickly. It did. I knew it was from God, and I cried. I always feel so humbled and in awe at His ability to work through me.

There were two problems that suddenly arose regarding this new song, "If I Could Just Phone Home." One was that I had just completed the long and costly process of recording my second CD, *Walk On*, not to mention that I needed to get it submitted for printing soon so that I could have it in time for Christmas deadlines. The second problem was cost. I just didn't think I could swing the payment for another song. I decided to leave it in God's hands by praying, "Okay, God. If this is really Your will that I add this song to my CD at this late date, then please help me write the music tomorrow, and let it flow quickly."

He did. The music came very easily, and so with joy, I added the song to the CD. Needless to say, however, I had never really gotten very much feedback from that particular song. It was strange. I couldn't imagine that something that felt "so from God" hadn't had a bigger impact than it did. I have learned however, that we don't always see the outcome of the seeds we have planted.

Recently, a woman whose relatives live in the apartment building with my mother, lost her seventeen-year-old autistic son, Alex. I had the opportunity to meet him several times, and he was just a big sweetheart. Always smiling. Always a kind word.

For some unknown reason, he just fell over and was gone instantly. A heart attack or aneurism was suspected. My own heart just ached for his family, and though I didn't know the mother well, I kept thinking that I would like to give her a copy of the song, "If I Could Just Phone Home." I kept putting it off, thinking it was too soon. Another time I would think about it and realize I didn't have her address. There were several times the idea would pop up, and I would say to myself, *I've got to get that song to Alex's mother!*

One morning after Mass, I stopped by to see my mother, and on the way, thought of taking the song over. I dismissed the thought when I realized that there was probably very little chance of seeing her that day, since I had only met her there a couple of times.

Sure enough, she walked into the apartment building. I excused myself from the group of residents who were sitting in the lobby having coffee and ran home to get it. I quickly printed off a copy of the words and headed back over to catch her before she left.

I wasn't even sure of her name, so I felt a little awkward. As I handed her the CD and the folded up words, I told her how sorry I was to hear of her son's passing and what a good young man she had raised. Tears filled her eyes as she thanked me and began talking about her pain.

Then she said something I will never forget. She patted her shirt pocket that held her cell phone and sadly said, "My phone used to ring all the time. I used to get calls many times a day from Alex. He would call me to tell me little things, like what he was eating, and . . . now . . . my phone . . . it never rings."

I could not believe my ears. I had not told her the name of the song. Tears welled up in my eyes as I marveled at God's goodness and mercy. I had just handed her a song entitled, "If I Could Just Phone Home." Through God's grace, this hurting mother and good Christian woman, was going to get her phone call after all.

It took an act of God for me not to just bawl openly right then. I stayed strong and told her the title of the song and why I gave it to her. She was very grateful and very touched.

Pondering things like this makes me sure that God's hand is, and always has been, in on everything good that I possess. I am also reassured that "There is an appointed time for everything. And a time for every event under heaven" (Ecclesiastes 3:1, NASB).

Is Eight Enough?

MARK ARMSTRONG

Remember the TV show *Eight Is Enough*? My wife, Patti, and I had enjoyed that show back in the seventies. By the nineties, we had eight children of our own. We thought it was enough.

Then our friend Evan paid us a visit. He came through town on sabbatical from his work as a missionary in Kisii, Kenya. We were expecting just to have dinner with him, but he was hoping for something more.

"Is there anything we could do for you?" I asked. I was thinking along the lines of a small donation or occasionally sending packages of goodies not available to him in Kenya.

A sly grin passed over his face. "Well," he began, "I have a bright young student who desperately wants to go to school in the United States. Would you consider taking him in?"

While Patti and I were recovering from the shock of being asked to take in a boy rather than send money or beef jerky, Evan elaborated.

"Calvin is a very good boy. His parents both died of

AIDS, and he was living with his two brothers. I found out he often went hungry and walked an hour and a half each way to school." Evan took a breath. He had our attention so he continued. "I invited him to stay at the school with me during the week so he can eat properly. He wanted me to bring him back with me, but I am seventy now so that would be impossible. I've been asking around in Bismarck to see if there is a family who might be willing to take Calvin into their home."

Calvin had our sympathy, but we already had eight children ranging from a one-year-old to a nineteen-year-old in college; six boys and two girls. "Even if we wanted to," Patti ventured, "we cannot afford one more."

Evan shrugged. "I know. That's why I was not planning to ask you. But after a few families suggested the Armstrongs, I thought I had to at least bring it up. One person thought that since you had so many kids already, maybe one more would not make much of a difference!" Patti and I looked at each other and smiled.

Then Evan suddenly brightened. "What if I got a family or two to help with the financial expenses?"

I loved being a father. So much of life was merely passing, but children were forever. It had always felt like an honor to me to be entrusted with God's little ones. The idea of becoming a father to an orphan intrigued me. I looked at Patti again. We knew each other well enough to know that the door to our hearts had opened just a crack.

In reality, no one really believed that Calvin would actually get permission to leave the country. At fifteen, he had no birth certificate. Before Evan left Bismarck, he had two families willing to help support Calvin and our promise to at least pray about it. Somehow we never actually got around to giving a bonafide yes. When Evan e-mailed us that Calvin had successfully gotten a birth certificate, the wheels were set in motion. But there were still a lot of hoops to get through. Terrorists had recently blown up the U.S. Embassy in Nairobi, so getting a passport and U.S. visa for an orphan to travel to the United States would not be easy. Everyone on all sides prayed, and with the help of a congressman in North Dakota, Calvin joined us in July of 2002. He easily became a part of our family. Our son Tyler, who is a month younger, quickly became best buddies with Calvin calling him, "his brother from the other color mother."

We thought we were being good Christians to take Calvin in, but when we heard the rest of the story, we realized it was we who had been blessed. God had chosen us to answer a special prayer that bordered on the miraculous.

Years earlier, Calvin gently closed his paperback novel as he lay in his mud hut. It was getting dark in the one-room home he shared with his two brothers. There was no money for oil to burn in their kerosene lantern, so reading needed to stop at sunset.

Ignoring the rumbling coming from his empty stomach, Calvin thought about the main character in his novel—a boy who left Africa to live with relatives in the United States and go to school there. "Maybe I could go there someday," Calvin dreamed.

"Dear God," he began praying. "Please let me go to school in the United States one day." Although it seemed that God had not answered so many of his prayers before, Calvin prayed with the trust of a child, even though at thirteen, his childhood seemed to have been lost long ago. Both his parents had died of AIDS, leaving Rogers, fifteen, Calvin, eleven, and Joash, nine, among Kenya's 650,000 AIDS orphans. The boys had loved their parents deeply. The ache caused by their absence overshadowed each day.

Relatives helped out a little, but as time went on, the assistance was gradually withdrawn. An uncle continued to pay the fees for him to attend school, but it was a long walk for Calvin from his hut to St. Patrick's Elementary School. Since he rarely had dinner the night before, his feet felt heavy as he trudged along. "If only I could go to school in the United States," Calvin began thinking on these long walks. And again, he would pray.

When Calvin revealed his prayer to his older brother and an aunt, he was laughed at. "You only own two pairs of pants and have no money," his aunt had laughed. "How do you think you are going to get to the United States?"

Rogers was sympathetic but no more encouraging. "Why don't you pray for something more practical like a bigger garden?" he had asked. The boys' only reliable source of food was a garden. It was not very big, but it provided vegetables around occasional donations of food from others.

Then, Evan Beauchamp came to work at the school as a missionary for the diocese of Bismarck, North Dakota. When he noticed that Calvin had a sore on his foot for several weeks that was not healing, he knew it must be the effects of malnutrition. He learned of the boy's hardships and invited Calvin to live with him during the school week and then return to help his brothers on the weekends. Calvin overflowed with appreciation. Not only would he receive better nutrition, but perhaps God was answering his prayer to eventually go to school in the United States.

It was not long before Calvin asked if perhaps Evan could take him back to the United States with him one day. Evan told him that would never be possible.

Calvin smiled as if he understood, but he kept praying and asking. Finally, Evan told Calvin he would ask his friends when he returned to the United States for his mid-service sabbatical the next year.

It was a month after Calvin joined us that we learned of his prayer. We were truly in awe at such faithfulness and to realize that God had picked our family to answer a young boy's prayers. Calvin is a much-loved member of our household. He and Tyler both graduated from high school with honors this year. Calvin was awarded a four-year scholarship to attend the University of Mary. He is determined to return to Kenya after graduation to help his countrymen in whatever way God leads him. It has been an honor to have Calvin call me Dad.

So, after Calvin joined our family, was nine finally enough? Well, we honestly thought so. Then, Evan hoped to have Calvin's younger brother, Joash, also come to school here. Again, he sheepishly asked us and again we said no . . . at first. After a lot of praying, we changed our minds and decided there was room for one more. Joash just finished his freshman year and is doing well. There's no more little brothers at home, so maybe ten is enough now. We will see.

Hillside Angel

SOPHIE MURDOCH

On school days Mom had our Chevy Suburban at her disposal. We needed room enough for us five kids, sacks of groceries, and whatever supplies the animals required. Our house in the Santa Barbara foothills sat on a high plateau with steep drop-offs front and back, reaching hundreds of feet down. We could see the entire city far below, but ours was like a place deep in the country. We had lots of animals running around—chickens, pigs, and of course our dogs and cats.

One late afternoon we headed up the three-mile dirt road to our house. Mom had picked me up after my piano lesson, and my brothers after soccer practice. I was eleven, Daniel was twelve, and Alex was nine. We'd also stopped off at the feed store for bags of grain for our chickens. "Quit bothering Chloe," I said to four-year-old Simon, scrunched in beside me. My baby sister was asleep in her car seat, but he liked to tickle the soft spot behind her ears. "You big kids unload the bags," my mother said. She backed the car up to the chicken coop.

"Okay, let's go," Mom said. Chloe was still asleep in her car seat. Daniel, Alex, and I climbed out, opened the rear door, and started unloading the grain. I heard Simon scrambling around inside the car. Everything was turning rosy red in the sunset. "Dad will be home soon," Mom said. "Let's hurry so I can start dinner." We were having my favorite, macaroni and cheese. *Thank you, God,* I thought. *Thank you for the best family in the world.*

I set down a bag of grain and turned to help Daniel with another. The car started to pull away from us. "Mom, wait!" I yelled. "We're not finished yet." But Mom wasn't in the driver's seat! There was noise behind me in the chicken coop: Mom appeared, her face white with shock. The Suburban rolled toward the edge of the precipice. The sun dipped behind the mountains. The sky went dark. The car disappeared over the hill.

Simon and Chloe! My brothers and I ran to the edge. Mom scrambled down, her dress parachuting behind her. I couldn't scream. I couldn't speak. The Suburban turned over, and the hood smashed against the ground. The front tires flew off. The car flipped again and again until it came to a crashing halt upright at the bottom of the hill. "I'm coming! I'm coming!" Mom cried.

Tears welled in my eyes. My legs were so weak that I could barely stand up, but my brothers and I ran down the dirt road. Mom stood by the car. Simon was at her side! "He's alive!" Mom cried. She had pulled him through the shattered windshield. But my heart stopped. I could see Chloe's car seat. It was still inside the car—empty.

Daniel knelt and held Simon. Mom tried to crawl through the shards of the rear window to search for Chloe. It was useless. My legs gave way, and I crumpled to my knees.

I bowed my head and prayed, but it was more with emotion than words. Simon was safe, but my baby sister could not have survived the accident without a miracle. I looked up. From my knees I could see under the Suburban. And I heard crying! Chloe! She lay in a hole in the ground just big enough to protect her.

Dad came home right away, and Mom drove Simon and Chloe to the hospital. We soon learned that the doctors in the emergency room were stupefied by my siblings. Simon had a scratch on his forehead, and Chloe a small cut on her shin. They came home with Band-Aids and a number to call in case of an emergency. A number that we never had to use.

I've heard people say they don't believe in miracles. How else can I explain what happened that day? Simon was shielded from the accident, and Chloe was carried from the car on protecting wings.

Thank you, God, for the best family in the world— and for Your angels, who hold us in their care.

Whispers of a Friend's Love

A friend loves you all the time, and a brother helps in time of trouble. (Proverbs 17:17, NCV)

Friends are truly blessings from God, and it is often through them that He sends us a word of encouragement, a helping hand, and yes, even a miracle. Who else would be more willing to be used by God for our uplifting than our friend and emotional brother or sister? From whom else would we be so willing to accept God's kindness and love than from our faithful friend? And so it is that often God's mercy and grace come to us as whispers of a friend's love.

Sometimes You Just Gotta Listen!

ELIZABETH J. SCHMEIDLER

The dog's out!"

I blew a gusty sigh from my lips as I watched my eight-year-old son, Paul, race outside to catch our dog. Cringing inwardly, I pictured our ninety-pound black Lab romping through the neighborhood at full speed, scaring little old ladies and innocent children simply by his massive size.

Stirring my boys' supper on the stove again, I turned the heat up a little, hoping to speed the process along. I glanced at the kitchen clock for the umteenth time and realized I was running just as late as the last time I'd looked. Feeling more than a little guilty, I grimaced, as I pictured my always-punctual husband waiting on me to finish getting ready . . . again. We were due to arrive at a banquet in less than an hour, and I was still dressed in my robe, with my just-shampooed hair wrapped in a towel. To soothe my conscience, I reminded myself that the phone had been ringing at a near constant rate all afternoon, which definitely had helped to add to my tardiness. Having a home-based candle business was a great way of earning extra money but certainly created extra commotion during the holiday season, which was now well under way.

If I can just get these noodles simmering, I can put on the lid and go get ready. I turned the heat under the skillet a little higher. Just then, my eldest son, Jerome signed for the delivery of ten cases of candles that the UPS man was getting ready to unload onto my kitchen floor via the garage door. I released yet another full-cheeked sigh and rolled my eyes as I realized that all ten cases would have to be tagged and marked before they could be put away. *It'll have to get done tomorrow,* I thought. *The customers will just have to wait.*

So as not to embarrass myself and shock the UPS man . . . or visa versa, I escaped from the kitchen and began to look for the dog out the bedroom window. As I stood there impatiently scanning the backyard, a tiny voice crept into my head. *Call Laura.* With a small shake of my head, I ignored the thought, gave up the window search, and proceeded to lay my clothes out onto the bed.

Call Laura. This time I argued with the thought. "Laura? Who's Laura?"

Ryan's mother. Ryan was the "new kid" in my son Paul's class. The boys had played together once, but I had actually spoken to Laura very little . . . mostly just short, friendly conversations while we passed each other in the parking lot at school. As I reached for my pantyhose, I remembered why I had let Paul go home with Laura the first time I met her . . . it was her smile and friendly face. Sounds naive, but true. I just knew, by way of a deep and peaceful instinct, that she was a good lady.

I suddenly recalled chatting with her briefly in the hall at school several days earlier. "We'll have to get together sometime! I'll call you," I remembered saying, as we shuffled along with the after-school rush to get outside.

Call Laura. I began yanking on my pantyhose, and inwardly vowed to call Laura soon and set up a lunch date or something fun. *Call Laura.* "OK, Lord, I'll call Laura later. Right now, I'm late!" I spoke aloud.

Just then, a waft of burning spaghetti sauce filled my nostrils. "Oh, noooo!" I exclaimed, as I envisioned the Hamburger Helper on its way to becoming "hamburger tartare." I rushed toward the kitchen and stumbled through the maze of boxes. After quickly turning the burner to low, I scraped at the gummy noodles that were now adhered to the bottom of the pan. Now I knew for sure—I was definitely having a Calgon moment.

"What next?" I mumbled, as my two-year-old son, Roy, tugged on my robe and asked me to read him a book. I managed a weak smile and answered, "I can't right now, sweetie. Mommy's very busy right now."

Call Laura.

"Please, Lord, I'll call her tomorrow . . . I *promise!*" Yet even as the words slipped from my lips, I knew the truth. God was trying to tell me something. This sort of inner calling had happened before, and I knew I should not ignore it.

Having gotten the dinner under control, I hoisted Roy onto my hip and went to look for the cordless phone. When I found it, I just stared at it. What would I say to her? *"Uh, Laura, this is Liz . . . yeah, Paul's mom. Remember me? Well . . . the strangest thing just happened . . . God told me to call you."* Oh, yeah, sure. *That would be perfect. She'll think I'm loony or something.*

I sighed and then looked up the number while popping a Barney video in the VCR for Roy to watch. One hand began applying my mascara, while the other dialed her number. As I listened to the ringing, I suddenly became apprehensive as to what I would say. *Maybe I should hang up.*

"Hello."

The mascara wand stopped, and I swallowed hard before saying, "Hi, Laura! This is Liz, Paul's mom. How are you?" I don't recall what she answered, since it took me just a split second to realize she was crying. I asked her what was wrong, and she explained that she had just found out that she had been pregnant for the very first time and had lost the baby. (They'd been blessed with Ryan through adoption.) To make matters worse, she had just been informed that she had developed an uncommon cancerous condition in her uterus that could be life threatening.

Suddenly, my predicament seemed petty. It didn't matter whether we would be late for dinner or whether someone would call the dogcatcher before we could lasso the dog and bring him home. I now cared very little if all the candles were put away before the customers arrived. I gripped the phone tightly and closed my eyes in a silent prayer.

When it was my turn to reply to her tearful declaration, I said, "I am so sorry for what you are going through, but I want you to know, you can stop crying because God has taken special care to have me call you tonight. I believe He wants you to know that He is present and in control of your situation. He cares about you very much and will not abandon you."

I then proceeded to tell her about the chaos in which I'd just ventured to call her. We laughed a little, and then talked with all seriousness about the truth. God had definitely placed her on my heart for a reason. I knew it, but more importantly, she knew it.

Like most people who are dealing with an illness or crisis, Laura went through some difficult times when she felt afraid. Sometimes I felt afraid for her. It was during these times that we would remind each other of the day that God whispered her name into my heart. In the months that followed, Laura's condition was healed completely! Best of all, we've been good friends and prayer buddies ever since!

By the way, in case you're wondering, the dinner tasted fine, the dog came back on his own to get a drink, and I actually was ready to go within minutes of my husband's arrival.

As the years go by, I marvel at the way God makes Himself known to us. I have learned to act quickly when He prompts me to do so, even when it's uncomfortable and hard. Even when He has called me to do something difficult, if I obey, I always end up feeling blessed beyond measure. He is Lord of all miracles, great and small.

The Voice of God

MARY HOLLINGSWORTH

Abilene Christian University is a relatively small school on the windswept plains of West Texas. Being on the only geographical rise in the area, folks in Abilene often refer to it as "holy hill." I was a senior in the early spring of 1970 and trying to decide what to do with the rest of my life.

In May I would receive my bachelor of science in business education degree, but by that time I had figured out I really liked writing, radio, and television. So I was planning to stay at ACU another year and work on my master's degree in journalism and mass communication. Meanwhile, I was working full time for the university in public relations, recruiting new students.

My interest in journalism had been piqued during my junior and senior years because I'd been working as a feature writer for the ACU student newspaper, the *Optimist*. It was really just for fun, and I'd enjoyed writing columns and articles in my spare time.

A requirement for entering the master's of communication program was to have a counseling meeting with a graduate advisor, who would help me fine-tune my degree plan and choose the right courses to prepare me for the career I hoped to pursue (whatever that was going to be). So the graduate administration office scheduled an appointment for me with Dr. Rex Kyker, chairman of the department, which I considered a great honor.

Dr. Kyker was an amazing man and respected by everyone who knew him. He was a robust man with a full shock of white hair, extremely articulate, brilliant, and kind. One of his daughters was in my class; so I decided he must be about my dad's age. At that particular time he was serving as president of Rotary International and was a highly sought-after speaker and presenter internationally. We were fortunate to get to hear him speak occasionally on campus, and I was always impressed with his wit, charm, and wisdom. He was also faculty supervisor of the *Optimist*.

When the scheduled time came, I was a little nervous about meeting with Dr. Kyker. I knew he would ask me what I wanted to do as a career, and I still wasn't really sure. I didn't want to sound like a wishy-washy student and be embarrassed, but I knew I had to be honest with him too. So I was muddling through what to say as I walked across campus to the administration building, went up to the second floor, and knocked on Dr. Kyker's door. His big, rich, deep voice responded, "Come on in, Mary!"

Opening the door, I was met by Dr. Kyker's welcoming smile and extended hand. "Sit down. Sit down. I've been looking forward to meeting you and getting to know you. I've admired the writing you've done for the *Optimist*." He immediately put me at ease.

I stammered a surprised thank-you and sat down across from him at his desk.

During our discussion that day, we were talking about whether I should complete my master's with an extra six hours of coursework or write a master's thesis. Dr. Kyker simply said, "You need to write a thesis, Mary, because you're going to be a writer."

I guess I nodded, because he wrote that down and we moved on to other things we needed to discuss. And even though we continued talking, I was in an emotional freeze-frame. *A writer? I'm going to be a writer? Why would he say that?* The idea had never crossed my mind before. Sure, I enjoyed writing articles for the student newspaper, and I'd worked on the annual staff in high school, but that was just for fun, wasn't it?

Thumbing through the pages of my memory, I also remembered entering writing contests in high school and even winning a few. But in those days, no one believed you could actually make a living as a writer. That was just something you did as a sideline, a hobby, in your spare time. No one finished the "great American novel" or became a famous writer—at least no one you knew.

Instead, I was encouraged to become a teacher—something stable that I could depend on through the years. So I did what everyone expected me to do and was getting a teaching degree. But about six weeks into my student teaching, I knew I didn't want to do this for the rest of my life. And I began thinking about what else I could do. Granted, it was a bit late in the game to be changing uniforms, but it was now or never. That's when I landed on the idea of pursuing a master's in communication, which would dovetail nicely with my business training and, perhaps, allow me to dabble in the communication arts.

At the end of my meeting with Dr. Kyker, I thanked him for his counsel and walked back to my dorm where I reviewed the notes I'd taken and began planning for the next year or two in grad school. And the thought crossed my mind again, *A writer? I wonder . . . .*

The next year was a blur as I worked full time and went to graduate school at night. It was a hectic time, and I was too focused on work and school to give Dr. Kyker's words much consideration, although occasionally his words "You're going to be a writer" darted through my mind and gave me pause. By the end of the year, I was ready to move on. But move on to what? Where did I want to go? And how would I get a job?

One day I ran into Dr. John Stevens in the hall of the administration building. Dr. Stevens was president of

ACU, and I'd gotten to know him while working with the dean of women on a special project for the university.

"Well, hello, Mary. How's it going?" he asked.

"Fine, Dr. Stevens. How about with you?"

"Everything's fine. Always busy at the end of the school year, of course. Say, what are you going to do now?"

I laughed and said, "I wish I knew. I've been trying to figure out where to get a job in the communications field, but so far I haven't come up with anything."

"Hmmmm," he said. "Would you be interested in the Dallas area?"

"Yes, I would. I have a lot of family and friends there, and it's not too far from my parents."

"Well, I have an idea. Come with me."

I followed Dr. Stevens to his big office in the corner of the administration building where he closed the door and asked me to sit down. I was a little intimidated by my surroundings, but he quickly took my mind off that by asking, "Have you ever heard of H. L. Hunt?"

"Is he the Hunt of Hunt's Catsup?"

"No," laughed Dr. Stevens. "He's the Hunt of Hunt Oil Company in Dallas. He may very likely be the wealthiest man in the world."

"Sorry. No, I don't know anything about him."

"Mr. Hunt has a large staff of people who work just for him, and I think you would be a good addition to his staff."

"Really? Well, I'm willing to work most anywhere. Since I don't know him, how would I approach him?" I asked.

"I can call him for you, if you'd like. In fact, I can call him right now."

"Oh. Well . . . all right. I guess that's fine."

"Now, Mary, if I call him, he'll ask me three questions. He'll want to know what you want to do, how much money you want to make, and when you can start. How would you answer those questions?"

At that moment, Dr. Kyker's words flashed through my mind: "You're going to be a writer."

Caught a bit off guard, I stuttered and said, "I'd really like to be a writer." Then I froze, thinking, *I can't believe I just said that.*

"What about the money?"

"I don't know, Dr. Stevens. What do you think would be fair?"

He said, "How about six hundred dollars a month?" (That was a lot of money to a new university grad in 1970.)

"That seems like a lot."

"Well, it's okay, because he's got a lot," he laughed. "And when do you want to start?"

"I have to finish this semester and my finals, but I could probably be there about June first."

"OK. Are you ready for me to make the call?"

Scared but hopeful I said, "I guess so."

Dr. Stevens dialed a number and waited for someone to answer. Now, I could only hear Dr. Stevens's side of the conversation; so this is what I heard:

"H. L., this is John Stevens at Abilene Christian University."

Pause.

"Yes, it's good to talk to you too. How's Ruth doing?"

Pause.

"Wonderful! I'm so glad to hear it. H. L., I'm calling you today because I have a very bright young woman here who would like to go to work for you."

Pause.

"Her name is Mary Shrode."

Pause.

"She wants to be a writer."

Pause.

"How about six hundred a month?"

Pause.

"She can be there on the first day of June."

Pause.

"No sir, she can't really get there any sooner."

Pause.

"Thank you, H. L., you'll be glad to have her on your staff. She'll do you a good job, and you can trust her."

Pause.

"Yes, the same to you. Good-bye."

Dr. Stevens hung up the phone and said to me, "OK, you're hired."

My mind was spinning. I couldn't believe how easy it was. And I could almost hear Dr. Kyker laughing and saying, "See, I told you, you're going to be a writer."

And that's exactly what I did. My first real job was to write political-comment columns for Mr. Hunt. They were syndicated under the title "Hunt for Truth" and read by millions of people every day across America. No one was more surprised by that turn of events than I.

Today I look back on my writing career with great humility. God has blessed me with more than ninety published Christian books. He has taken my tiny talent and my stubby pencil and used them for His own glory. What more could I possibly want to do with my life?

Over time I have come to know that the voice I heard so many years ago say, "You're going to be a writer," wasn't really the voice of Rex Kyker at all. It was the voice of God whispering in my ear through a friend what He knew in advance He was going to do with me. And I will be eternally grateful.

27 Steps

IRENE GUBRUD

In Minneapolis's Orchestra Hall the curtain is up for the July 1977 Tchaikovsky Festival. An audience of three thousand people is waiting. And I tremble.

An awesome expanse of stage gleams before me. It stretches from where I stand in the wings to a writing desk out on center stage where I will sing "Tatiana's Letter Scene" from Tchaikovsky's opera, *Eugene Onegin*.

I know exactly how far away that desk is. Twenty-seven steps.

Twenty-seven steps. A quick walk from the kitchen to the living room for most people. For me it will be like climbing Mount Everest.

For eighteen years I have been handicapped, ever since the age of twelve when in 1959 a defective carnival ride hurled me sixty feet through the air to the concrete pavement. I lay unconscious for three days and nights, and it wasn't until several weeks after regaining consciousness that I realized I was unable to move my legs. The doctors held the gray X-ray films to the light and pointed to crushed vertebrae and a damaged spinal cord. A neurosurgeon told my mother that I would never get out of a wheelchair.

Never walk? Never water ski? Never jump and prance as a cheerleader for Canby Junior High?

I couldn't believe it, and at first, I wouldn't believe it. But after five months in the hospital, when the therapist clamped the leather and steel braces on my legs, the truth sank in. I hoisted myself up on forearm crutches, stared at the ugly braces, and burst into tears.

After four more months of therapy, I was able to swing along quickly on crutches. Later, I learned to get by with ankle supports instead of leg braces. I could even work my way up and down stairs. But my dream of walking was shattered. In the backs of my thighs and from the knees down there was no usable muscle. My feet hung loose like limp flags. It was a condition the therapists called "foot drop."

Soon after entering St. Olaf College, I felt that I had found my true calling. I had a voice. A really good voice. Music had always been part of my family's life, and I had played a flute and piano besides singing as a soloist since I was a youngster. At a freshman talent night, I finished my aria from *Madama Butterfly* and the audience rose for a five-minute standing ovation. Exhilarated, I returned to my dorm to sit before the mirror and dream of the future. Was I being called to become a singer?

In my prayers that night I asked God to guide me, to let me know somehow whether I should pursue singing as a career. The next day I discussed my dream with my college voice teacher. "You have the potential of becoming a beautiful lyric soprano," she told me. "Your voice has a richness, a radiant quality."

I concentrated on my lessons, practicing daily. I studied French and Italian.

At the end of my freshman year I applied for the college choir. The director called me in for a talk, and I eagerly settled at his desk, leaning my crutches against the wall. He looked down as if struggling to find words, then gently told me that—though I had a beautiful voice—I would not be in the choir.

"Why?" I asked in astonishment.

"The group goes on three-week tours," he explained, slowly tapping a pencil on his desk. "The students sing every night and often have to stand for hours."

He looked up apologetically. "Besides," he added, "we have to be able to get on and off the stage quickly."

I struggled to my feet and made my way back to my car where I laid my head on the steering wheel and cried.

Choir or no choir, I went on singing through college whenever and wherever—in churches, in student assemblies. I went on with my voice lessons and studied music, history, diction, and dramatization, working hard and faithfully. Upon graduation with a bachelor of music degree in voice I won a scholarship to the Juilliard School of Music in New York. I studied harder still, month after month, also learning Russian diction on my own, in addition to taking private voice lessons. Then I sang for the first time before professional critics in the Concert Artists Guild contest. Winning that competition led directly to my concert debut at New York's Carnegie Recital Hall, and that in turn to engagements with major symphony orchestras around the country. I thought my career was about to blossom. In the spring of 1972 I decided I was ready to enter the annual student auditions for training by the Metropolitan Opera Company of New York.

I sang well in that audition, and I knew it. For a week I waited for word. Finally I was called into the offices at the Met. I settled into a chair, tucking my crutches on the floor beside me, and looked into a sympathetic face.

It was a horrible experience of déjà vu.

"Miss Gubrud, it's your disability. We feel you would not be able to handle opera." The kindly voice went on about how opera singers have to be able to walk on the stage. "So in all fairness to you," came the conclusion, "we must disqualify you from the audition."

Again I was crushed. It didn't matter that the Met gave me a scholarship and wanted me to sing in studio concerts where I would not have to walk around; I had my heart set on opera. Unwilling to give up, I traveled about auditioning for other opera companies that fall. Again and again it was the same answer: "You have a strong, clear young voice, but because of your crutches . . ."

Finally, I had to accept reality. It was obvious that there was no reasonable way for me to appear in an opera, no matter how well I sang.

But now, at twenty-five, I grew desperate. Where would I find work? Unlike the many concertos that exist in orchestras and ensembles for instrumental soloists, there are few openings for a soprano outside of opera. Was I going to have any kind of career at all?

"I don't know what to do, Lord." I prayed. "You must have given me this voice to be used. Please help me know what to do with my future."

I tried hard to listen. Slowly, but unmistakably, it became very clear to me. If I was going to do anything with my life, I had to walk without crutches, impossible as it might seem.

I started by seeing a chiropractor and a therapeutic masseur six times a week. Both of them helped, removing some of the tension in my body. Still seeking, I consulted an acupuncturist, who stimulated some nerve activity.

Then in 1974 came a breakthrough.

A friend told me about a minister who was to be a

guest speaker at a church in Hartford, Connecticut. She said his name was John Scudder. He had once been an aeronautical engineer, but had given himself completely to the Lord and now was a pastor of a church in Illinois.

"He has a healing ministry, Reenie," said my friend. "Maybe he can help you."

Intrigued, I went to Connecticut to hear him talk. He was tall and thin, and there was a special presence about him. He spoke of an abundant life through living in accordance with the teachings of Christ. "God wants us to be whole," he emphasized. "The trouble is that too many of us fail to believe it."

After his talk, I went up to him and confessed my dream of walking again. "Could you help me?" I asked.

I'll never forget his answer. "Do you believe in the power of God?"

"Oh yes," I said.

From then on John Scudder became my teacher, not only in spiritual guidance but in physical therapy through special exercises he prescribed.

In 1975, a year later, I moved to Illinois, where his wonderful wife and two children welcomed me into their family. There I continued with the therapy sessions designed to rebuild my leg muscles, practiced my music daily, and filled singing engagements around the country. I also helped Mrs. Scudder with the house, including aiding with the family's voluminous correspondence.

Paramount in everything from day to day, of course, was prayer. "Remember," John Scudder reminded me over and over, "with faith in Him there is nothing you can't do."

When I became impatient with the sessions, he'd say, "None of us knows how long it will take for you to walk, Reenie, but we all must learn to go beyond setting time limits. Just to know, to believe that it will happen through Him, is all that is necessary."

Gradually, my knee-bend and leg-lift exercises became easier; my limbs were getting stronger.

"Therapy is all well and good," John would say. "But the time will come when you'll have to place your trust in God—your complete trust."

He often reminded me of the time in old Jerusalem when critics accused Jesus of making Himself equal to God. Our Lord replied, "The Son can do nothing of Himself, but what He seeth the Father do" (John 5:19, KJV).

"Think of the miracles that Jesus wrought, of His perfection," said John, "and yet He had the humility to admit that of Himself He could do nothing."

In time I came to know without a doubt that God would work through me if I allowed Him to.

In June 1977 after two years of therapy and prayer, John said to me, "It is time for you to walk."

I trembled but knew he was right. Some time before I had accepted an offer to sing as soloist in the Minnesota Orchestra's Tchaikovsky Festival scheduled to take place just three weeks hence. I had already been rehearsing for it. Now I faced a dilemma: I wanted to walk, but was it wise to begin such strenuous exercises while practicing my music?

My faith was still a bit shaky. *Can I do it?* I wondered. I wanted to try. To begin, I enlisted the help of Joe and Jackie, two close friends my age from John Scudder's church. Early one evening we drove to a suburban shopping center where there was a secluded area behind the buildings, I got out of the car. This time I left my crutches behind. With Jackie and Joe supporting me, I began "walking" along between them. My legs felt like spaghetti, but I went through the motions for an hour. Each day we increased the "walking" by twenty minutes, until the three of us were walking for two hours.

After four days Jackie said, "Okay, tomorrow night you'll walk alone."

I was thunderstruck. "Without you holding me?"

"Yes."

"But, Jackie, I can't. Please, if you love me, don't make me do that."

"It's just because we love you, Reenie, that we are," said Joe. "We've put in a lot of time for you; now you're going to have to do this for us."

I meekly agreed.

On a clear summer evening, I stepped out of the car, my friends supporting me. We walked a few feet and then they backed away. I lifted my right foot, tottered a few steps and fell to the ground.

Jackie and Joe helped me to my feet. "Congratulations, you took three steps!' Jackie exclaimed.

"Let's do it again," I said determinedly. Breathing deeply, I stood looking into the mauve twilight. My heart pounded.

I breathed a prayer. "Father, I know it is impossible for me to walk alone. But with You . . ."

I took a step. The ground swayed and I tottered. But, arms flailing, I balanced and put the other foot forward. Again and again. Five steps, six, seven . . . and I fell.

Jackie and Joe rushed up. I shook my head. "No, I have to get up by myself!"

I struggled to my feet. My knee stung from the fall. My temples throbbed from the effort.

Again I put one foot in front of the other, ten steps, fifteen, nineteen! I collapsed again and struggled to my feet. My steps were awkward, and each one required tremendous effort. This time I was able to walk a full two minutes. It had finally happened. I had walked free of crutches for the first time in eighteen years!

My heart overflowing with gratitude, I decided to walk on that stage in Minnesota, back home where it all began.

Now it is two weeks later in Minneapolis, and I wait

in the wings for the concert performance of *Eugene Onegin* to begin. Andre Kostelanetz, the conductor, stands behind me. There is applause. I look out at the twenty-seven steps to center stage. I had walked this distance and more in the shopping center. And I have already practiced on this stage with the auditorium empty.

But can I do it amid the excitement of all those people? Will I stumble? Fall? Three thousand wait quietly in the audience. My mother and family are there. John Scudder and his family are there. And Jackie and Joe.

I get my cue. I breathe a prayer. The auditorium is still. I lift my left foot.

Three steps . . . four . . . five . . . I fasten my eyes on the writing desk.

Hands begin to patter in the dark.

I walk on, perspiration building under my makeup. The patter swells into loud clapping. The desk looms closer.

Now the audience is on its feet, the auditorium reverberating with a deafening roar,

I reach center stage, and, my hand resting on the polished mahogany desk, I turn and face the audience. Then I sing. I sing for them and for God, for the One through Whom all things are possible, the One Who has caused the lame and the halt to rise up and walk.

In Limbo

LONNIE ORFITELLI

My eyes slowly adjusted to the dim light. I had been to enough high-school dances to recognize the scene: the basketball hoops hung with crepe paper, wrestling mats rolled up beneath the bleachers, a big painted Go Wildcats! sign on one wall. The students milled around in tight groups, ignoring the deejay who tried to cajole everyone into dancing.

"Hey, Lon," my friend Greg shouted. It was his high school, and he thought I'd enjoy coming. He slapped me on the back and introduced me to his group. But soon they were caught up in a conversation about their football team, their teachers, and who was going steady. I didn't have anything to say. When the deejay made another appeal for everyone to twist and shout, the guys crossed the gym, joining a group of girls on the other side, leaving me alone.

Leaning against the cold brick wall, I watched Greg grab one girl's hand and step out on the dance floor. I felt awkward at my own school dances, a lowly freshman without a girlfriend. But at least there I had a few buddies to commiserate with. Here I stood by myself and moved my head back and forth in time to the music. Gazing up at the gym clock in its big metal cage, I started to count the minutes. How much longer before I could leave without looking like a complete jerk?

"All right, all right, Wildcats," the deejay said. "It's time for Chubby Checker's latest tune. Clear the floor. I want only the top cats to compete. Let's have a limbo contest!"

There was a smattering of applause as several older guys in skinny ties and baggy chinos stepped forward. "Go to it!" someone shouted. Using a broom, I had practiced the limbo with my sisters for hours at home. Now I stepped out to center court. "I'd like to try," I said, surprising myself.

The new Chubby Checker hit came on and each of us went under the bar. With each round it came down a notch. The music got louder and the room got hotter as our shrinking group of contestants staggered around in a circle, dropping down at the bar and lowering ourselves under. Other kids clapped, shouting encouragement. Soon there were only ten of us. I was in the finals! I looked around for Greg. Where was he? Where had he gone?

The sweat dripped down my arms as I lowered myself beneath the bar. Nine, eight, seven, six—one by one the others were eliminated. A tall guy with pointed black shoes dipped in front of me, and then he faltered. The bar tumbled down. He was out. I went next, slithering under. No problem.

By the time the music came to a stop I was amazed. I had finished in fourth place. A gray-haired chaperone presented me with a huge bag of candy. Then I dashed to wash my face. As I bent over the sink, I kept telling myself, *You're a winner, you're a winner.* I couldn't believe it. I had done it.

While I was staring into the mirror, the door opened and four upperclassmen barged in, glaring at me. I immediately recognized the guy with the pointed black shoes. I turned around and glanced at my bag of candy sitting on the floor.

"You have something that belongs to my friend," said one of the fellows, a hulking figure in a jacket and chinos.

The leader swaggered over and leaned his face close to mine. He shoved my shoulder. "Now, about the candy . . . "

"You c-c-c-can have it," I stammered, thinking, *Greg, where are you?*

Just then the bathroom door swung open, and a tall athletic fellow stepped in. "Lon," he said to me, "great to see you, buddy." I stared blankly at the black stranger who parted the wall of bullies surrounding me. He shook my hand and put his arm around my shoulder.

"Glad to have you here tonight," he said. "It's been a long time."

My new "friend" turned around and looked squarely at each guy. "You'll excuse us, fellows, won't you? Lon and I have some catching up to do." Although he spoke politely, his demeanor left no room for discussion.

The group of four stepped backward and allowed us to pass. I picked up my candy, and with his arm around my shoulder, my friend steered me out the door ahead of him. We stepped into the gym. The pressure of his arm disappeared. At the same moment, he vanished into the dancing crowd.

Later I found Greg and showed him my prize—he'd been outside getting some fresh air during the limbo contest. "I'm sorry," he said. "I guess I wasn't a very good friend."

"That's okay," I told him. "I made a new friend tonight." A friend I'd never seen before and have never seen since. Somehow, though, I believe if I'm really in trouble, I'll see him—or another just like him—again.

The Truest of Friends

NANCY SULLIVAN

I pulled the pink envelope from our mailbox just as my daughter was coming home from school. It looked like a birthday party invitation. "SARAH" was carefully printed in bold, black letters. When Sarah stepped off the bus I tucked the envelope into her hand. "It's . . . it's . . . for me," she stuttered, delighted.

In the unseasonably warm February sun we sat down on the front porch. As I helped her open the envelope, I wondered who had sent it. Maybe Emily or perhaps Michael, pals from her special-education class.

"It's . . . it's . . . from Maranda!" Sarah said, pointing to the front of the card. There, framed with hearts, was a photo of a girl I had never seen before. She had beautiful long hair, a dimpled grin, and warm smiling eyes. "Maranda is eight years old," the caption read. "Come and celebrate on Valentine's Day."

Glancing at the picture, I felt uneasy. Clearly, Maranda was not handicapped. Sarah, on the other hand, had Down syndrome and was developmentally delayed in all areas. At age nine she still functioned on a preschool level. Her disability was obvious, marked with thick-lensed glasses, a hearing aid, and stuttering.

A happy child, she had many friends who used wheelchairs and braces and walkers. But this was the first time she had been invited to the home of a nondisabled child. "How did you meet Maranda?" I asked.

"At . . . at . . . school. We eat lunch together every . . . every day."

Even though Sarah was in special education she socialized with other second graders during gym, lunch, and homeroom. I had always hoped she would make friends outside her program. Why, then, did I feel apprehensive?

Because I'm her mother, I thought. I loved Sarah. I wanted and prayed that she would have the best. I also knew a friendship with Sarah called for extra sensitivity, tolerance, and understanding. Was the child in the photo capable of that?

Valentine's Day came. Sarah dressed in her favorite pink lace dress and white patent leather shoes. As we drove to Maranda's party she sat next to me in the front seat, clutching the Barbie doll she had wrapped with Winnie-the-Pooh paper and masking tape. "I . . . I'm so excited," she said.

I smiled, but deep inside I felt hesitant. There would be other children at the party. Would they tease Sarah? Would Maranda be embarrassed in front of her other friends? *Please, Lord,* I prayed, *don't let Sarah get hurt.*

I pulled into the driveway of a house decorated with silver heart-shaped balloons. Waiting at the front door was a little girl in a red sweater trimmed with ribboned hearts. It was Maranda. "Sarah's here!" she called. Racing to our car, she welcomed my daughter with a wraparound hug. Soon seven giggling girls followed Maranda's lead, welcoming Sarah with smiles.

"Bye, Mom," Sarah said, waving as she and the others ran laughing into the house. Maranda's mother, Mary, greeted me at my rolled-down car window.

"Thanks for bringing Sarah," she said. "Maranda is so excited Sarah could come to her party." Mary went on to explain that her daughter was an only child and that Maranda and Sarah had become special friends at school. "Maranda talks about her all the time," she said.

I drove away, amazed. Still, I couldn't get over my uneasiness. Could this friendship ever be equal? Maranda would need to learn the language of Sarah's speech. She would need patience when Sarah struggled with certain tasks. That was a lot to ask of an eight-year-old.

As the months passed I watched the girls' friendship grow. They spent many hours together in our home. Fixing dinner in the kitchen, I heard giggles fill the family room as they twirled around an old recliner or watched *The Lion King*. Other times they dressed up in my old hats and outdated blouses, pretending to be famous singers. Soon the months turned to years.

One afternoon in late autumn, 1995, I watched the two of them sitting next to each other at our kitchen table. Sarah held a pencil; Maranda had a tablet of paper.

Maranda called out each letter as she guided Sarah's hand: "S-A-R-A-H." Though some of the letters had been printed backward or upside-down, Maranda praised Sarah's effort. "Great job," she said, applauding.

At Christmastime the girls exchanged gifts. Sarah gave Maranda a photograph of herself, a framed first-communion picture. "You look beautiful," Maranda said as she admired Sarah's white ruffled dress and long lace veil. In return, Maranda gave Sarah a gray-flannel elephant trimmed with an "I love you" tag. It quickly became Sarah's favorite stuffed animal, and she slept with it every night.

A few weeks into the new year Sarah came home from school looking downcast. "M-Maranda is . . . is sick," she said. I thought maybe she had caught the bug circulating at school. Minutes later, however, Sarah's special-education teacher called. Maranda was in the hospital. She had sustained a seizure at school and had been diagnosed with a brain tumor. Surgeons had performed a risky operation, which had left Maranda paralyzed on one side with impaired speech and vision. The biopsy results weren't back yet.

"Can we visit her?" I asked. I knew Sarah would want to see her friend.

"Maranda is very despondent and not up to seeing anybody," the teacher told me. "Her parents are requesting cards rather than visits."

"We'll keep her in our prayers," I promised.

That night Sarah knelt beside her bed, clutching her stuffed elephant. "Please ma . . . ma . . . make Maranda better," she prayed. Night after night she implored God to heal her friend. Then one night in early February Sarah stopped abruptly in the middle of her prayer. She nudged me.

"Let's ma . . . ma . . . make a valentine for Ma . . . Maranda."

The next day we sat together at the kitchen table as I helped Sarah write Maranda's name on a large sheet of pink-and-white construction paper. She decorated each letter with stickers and glittery Magic Markers. She drew a large heart around the name, then glued candy hearts with phrases like "friends forever" and "be mine." In similar fashion she added four more pages. Just before we slid the card into a large envelope, Sarah asked, "How . . . how . . . how do I spell love?" I called out the letters as she painstakingly printed "LOVE," the letters crooked and out of place, followed by her name.

Two weeks passed. We heard that Maranda had

additional surgery. On Valentine's Day I got a phone call from her mother. "Maranda's home," she said, "and wants to see Sarah."

"Home?" I asked with surprise.

"Maranda's tumor was benign. We're hoping for a full recovery."

As we discussed Maranda's prognosis, she relayed how thankful she was for Sarah and her card. "Maranda was very depressed. She had stacks of letters, cards, and gifts, but wouldn't open any of them. Then one morning Sarah's homemade card arrived. We opened it, and Maranda burst into a huge smile. She hugged it and wouldn't put it down." Mary's voice was choked with emotion. "It was an answer to prayer."

I realized then that Sarah and Maranda were the truest of friends. Their bond was defined not by intellect or health or handicap, but by love, unconditionally given and received. They had overcome disability with laughter and support. Their friendship had always been equal.

Today both girls are doing well. Maranda is almost twelve and Sarah is going on thirteen. With the help of intensive therapy Maranda's neurological functions returned to normal, and Sarah's speech has improved immensely. She can even read some. Though we've moved to a different neighborhood, the girls still keep in touch. Recently Maranda came to sleep over.

As the girls sat at our kitchen table they talked about

Maranda's newly pierced ears and Sarah's "secret" boyfriend from her special-ed class. Then in the middle of their conversation Sarah opened a kitchen drawer and pulled out a tablet and pencil.

"S-A-R-A-H," Maranda called out, just like old times. As Sarah printed her name without any help, Maranda looked on and clapped. "Great job, Sarah!" she said. I took a peek at my daughter's masterpiece. Her name had been written perfectly.

CHAPTER 4

Reaching Out in Love

This royal law is found in the Scriptures: "Love your neighbor as you love yourself." If you obey this law, you are doing right. (James 2:8, NCV)

Have you ever noticed that reaching out in love to touch the life of someone else has a ripple effect? It makes that person want to reach out and help someone too. And the ripple goes ever outward, like those caused by dropping a stone in a mirrored lake. Is it any surprise then that God Himself often drops the first stone by reaching out in love to touch us?

The A Cappella Angel

MARY HOLLINGSWORTH

In the summer of 1991 our church choir—The Richland Hills Family Singers—traveled to Ireland and Scotland on a fourteen-day mission outreach concert tour. Our purpose was to visit small churches and communities to bring them the gospel story in song and to encourage Christians and missionaries in those countries.

Our travel and concert schedule was packed, with very little lag time during the days and evenings. We often did two or three concerts in one day and had to stay on a strict schedule in order to get from one to the next in a timely way.

The Family Singers numbered around forty, as well as several spouses and others who traveled with us to assist with distributing programs, setting up our risers, keeping track of our personal belongings during concerts, and myriad other details involved with administering a group that size.

Our mode of transportation was a huge fifty-four-seat tour bus, complete with a professional driver and highly experienced tour guide named Victoria. Her job was constant and complicated, keeping up with our large troop, and she did it well.

About four days into the tour, we were scheduled to present an evening concert at St. Mary's Church in a small Irish town. The concert was at 7:00; so we arrived about 5:30 in order to prepare for the performance, warm up in the building, and get used to the acoustics (which can vary greatly in European churches and cathedrals). We had already checked into our hotel for the night, had an early dinner, and changed into our formal attire; so we were all set to perform.

Expecting to be met by our hosts at St. Mary's, we were surprised when the huge cathedral on the edge of town was locked, the lights were off, and no one was around. A couple of our leaders went searching for someone to open the building and came back eventually with a janitor, who was obviously *not* expecting us and knew nothing of our concert in just over an hour. However, he graciously opened the building for us and left.

While we were rehearsing, Victoria and the bus driver locked the bus and walked down the street to have dinner. We didn't know where they went, but we knew they would be back just in time for the concert, as was their custom.

Around 6:30 we began growing concerned, because our hosts had still not appeared, and no audience was assembling in the big auditorium. So, once again, we sent a couple of emissaries to see who they could find and check out the situation. They were gone for almost twenty minutes, and our director, Charlotte, was beginning to panic in earnest. It was now ten minutes until seven.

Finally, the two guys returned with a little, old nun in tow. She was shaking her head, saying quietly to Charlotte that she didn't understand. They had no knowledge of our concert and were certainly unprepared to host one.

"Besides," she said with confidence, "if our community knew that a wonderful American choir like yours was performing at St. Mary's, this cathedral would be completely full by now. Are you sure you are in the right place?"

"Yes," said Charlotte, "our itinerary shows that we are to sing at St. Mary's Church at 7:00 P.M. tonight."

"St. Mary's *Church?*" asked the nun with a suddenly enlightened expression.

"Yes, that's right."

"Well, that explains it, then," smiled the nun. "We are St. Mary's *Cathedral*. St. Mary's *Church* is about ten minutes from here on the downtown square. You're in the wrong place!"

"Oh no!" Charlotte almost shouted. "We have to get there immediately! Thank you for your help."

And turning to us, she said, "We're at the wrong church, folks! Grab everything and let's go!"

Well, talk about mass chaos! We basically ran out of the cathedral to the bus. But the bus was still locked, and Victoria and the driver were nowhere in sight.

"Where did they go to dinner?" asked Charlotte.

No one knew. Now what?

Meanwhile, Lee Nelson, one of our leaders, had spotted another large tour bus parked behind ours. The driver was sitting at the wheel, munching on an apple.

Lee got his attention, and he opened his window.

"Sir, we have a major panic on our hands, and we need help. I have fifty people who are supposed to be at St. Mary's Church about ten minutes from here *right now* giving a concert, but we're at the wrong church. Our bus driver and guide have locked our bus and gone somewhere to dinner, but we don't know where. Is there any way you can help us?"

"Well, I sure can. Climb aboard, laddie, and I'll take you there meself."

The Family Singers clambered onto this bus of mercy, dragging all our gear and belongings with us. Lee left a note on the window of our bus for Victoria, and the bus driver took off across town at record speed.

We arrived at St. Mary's Church about ten minutes late to find a full house waiting patiently for our arrival. Seeing the large crowd already in place, Charlotte made a fast decision. We quickly lined up in our procession order and immediately walked in from the back of the church singing our first number (the advantage of being an a cappella choir!). We continued to sing as we arranged ourselves properly on the steps of the podium at the front of the sanctuary. It worked out so perfectly that it looked as if we had planned and practiced it that way. And the acoustics of that historic old wooden church were so fine that we didn't even need our sound equipment.

About ten minutes into our concert, which went extremely well after that, Victoria and the bus driver came hurrying into the back of the auditorium with panicked expressions. Seeing that all was well, they sat down for the remainder of the program.

The audience was entirely gracious, giving us a standing ovation and inviting us to join them for a devotional after the concert. It was a wonderful time of interaction and worship. And the evening turned out to be one of our favorite memories.

Apologizing to Charlotte after the program, Victoria said with a red face, "It's surely the first time I've ever lost my entire tour group!"

As we left the church, Victoria asked Lee about the other bus that had brought us across town. Lee gave her the name of the bus company and the driver's name. She stopped and asked him to repeat the information, which he did.

"You know, Lee, I've been a tour guide on this small island for more than twenty-five years. I know *all* the tour companies and every driver in Ireland, but I've never heard of that tour company or driver . . . ever."

Lee began asking the rest of us to confirm the name of the bus and driver, which we did. And Victoria just shook her head, saying again, "There is no such tour company or driver in Ireland. I'm absolutely positive of that."

The next day Victoria called the Irish agency that oversees the tour companies, and they confirmed that there was and never had been any such company or driver in all of Ireland. And we were all baffled by the news.

For the next few days as we continued our tour through Ireland, we kept our eyes peeled for that wonderful bus of mercy and its kind driver, but we never saw it or him again. Nor have we heard anything else about them to this day.

So, who was that driver, and why was he sitting there in an empty tour bus outside the *wrong* church at just the *right* moment? Why did he immediately agree to take us across town, and then how did he disappear so completely?

The Family Singers think we know, and we have thanked God for him many times since then. To us, he is the A Cappella Angel, who reached out to a group of strangers in our time of need.

Sarah's Story

LOU KILLIAN ZYWICKI

From the day she entered my eleventh-grade classroom, Sarah Smith did nothing but glare. At me, at
other students. She refused to participate in class and
wouldn't speak when spoken to. (Though she did know
how to swear.) She refused to call me by name, instead
shouting out, "Hey, you!"

I'd been teaching English for twelve years at the
Duluth Secondary Technical Center, a vocational high
school in Minnesota, and I liked to think I had a way
with students. But with Sarah, I was lost. Some mornings I'd send her to the hallway, hoping a few minutes
alone would cool her temper. But it never did.

Still, there was something about her that tugged at
my heart. I knew she was a foster child who'd been
banged around by life. I knew that so often, especially
in kids, anger sprang from fear. I believed God led me
to teaching so he could use me to reach kids like Sarah,
to make a difference in their lives. I'd never given up
on a student yet. But after one particularly trying class,

I bowed my head in prayer. *Lord, I don't know what to do. Help me find the key to Sarah's heart.*

Soon after, her foster mother came to see me. Sarah was just as difficult at home as she was at school.

"Last night she didn't want the hot dogs I cooked, so she threw them against the wall," Mary Kelly said.

Like me, Mary was at her wit's end.

"Tell me what you know about her," I said. "Between the two of us, maybe we can find a way to reach her."

She told me Sarah's story. "Sarah was living in a Dumpster when our church outreach program found her," Mary said. "She couldn't go home; her mother was an alcoholic. One night while Sarah was sleeping, her mother burned her back with a cigarette. My pastor asked if I'd take her. He knew how lonely I'd been since my husband died, and he knew I had an extra room."

I took a deep breath. "She must have dreams," I said. "All kids do."

"I don't know if she does," Mary said. "Sarah says she's never been a success at anything. Each day I pray she'll find one thing she can be good at. Just one thing."

Just one thing. I turned to the blackboard. That day I'd written an announcement about the annual northern Minnesota essay contest. There's a grand-prize winner and one runner-up. Thousands enter from across the state. Each year I challenge my students to write stories, and many usually do.

Now, for some reason, I blurted, "Let's pray Sarah enters the contest." As soon as the words left my mouth I had second thoughts. I had no idea if Sarah could write, let alone write an essay. Here was a child who could barely communicate. Was an invitation to enter this contest simply an invitation to fail?

But Mary loved the idea. "I'm going to go home and tell Sarah," she said.

Before class the next morning Sarah shuffled into my room and tossed a smeared sheet onto my desk.

"You gonna learn me how to win that contest?" It was the first full sentence I'd heard her speak, more or less.

I quickly scanned her story. *Oh, Lord,* I thought. *Oh no. She can't write at all.* "Raw" was the best adjective I could find. Raw at best but largely incomprehensible to anyone who didn't know Sarah.

"Sit down, please," I said. Sarah plopped down at a desk in a kind of sullen slouch. I sat beside her. Sarah's eyes bore into me, as if daring me to utter any critical word.

"There's a lot of real emotion here," I began. "I sense you're trying to write about your life . . . who you are and why. But a good story has to have more than sheer emotion. You need some structure . . ."

Sarah rose and without a word stalked out the door, glaring as she went. Had she heard a word I'd said? Even the good ones?

She was early again the next morning. She tossed a new version of her story onto my desk and waited, tapping her foot as I read. Frankly, it was painful, both subject matter and the telling. This time I tried to teach her about dialogue. I gave her an excerpt from an Elmore Leonard novel where the dialogue sang. Again, without a word, she got up and left. I reread her story and made a mental note to fit a grammar lesson into our next class.

Morning after morning Sarah flung a new version of her story onto my desk. Then she'd wait, glaring and tapping her foot. Each night at home I'd dig through all of my creative-writing magazines, searching for tips on how to teach her the art of storytelling. Every night I said a prayer, *Please help me reach Sarah!*

In her way Sarah was reaching out too. In class she still glared at any student who looked in her direction. She still refused to answer when called on. And she persisted in calling me "Hey, you." But she did her homework now and did well enough on tests. She even swore less.

Then, after six weeks, a story began to emerge. A strong story with a compelling protagonist, rising action, realistic dialogue. The raw emotion was there too, but more controlled. Was Sarah learning to rein in the emotion of her own life by learning to handle it in a piece of fiction?

One morning I sat her down. "You've really got something here. You've developed a strong voice and an original style." It was the first time I didn't have to struggle to find something to compliment her about.

Sarah's eyes lit up. "My story isn't going to be a common story, ma'am."

Ma'am? What happened to "Hey, you?" I took a chance. I probed into her life. "Where does this story come from?"

"It comes from being unloved," Sarah said. "From no one believing in you."

"Look around you," I said. "Your foster mom. Me. We believe in you, Sarah."

"It's hard to trust people," she said, shaking her head. "They let you down."

But as Sarah gained confidence in her writing, I saw her beginning to try to trust. One day, after a few students read their story drafts aloud, she raised her hand. "I want to read mine." Sarah opened her notebook and began. The room fell silent. Her story was powerful. It touched everyone.

On deadline day I bundled my students' entries and mailed them in. I was proud of Sarah's story, but I knew it didn't stand a chance. It was still too raw, too unformed. That will be her next lesson. Handling rejection. I knew it would hurt. Maybe too much. That night I called the contest director, a man I'd known for years.

"Mike, I need a favor." I told him Sarah's story.

"This kid has faced stuff no child should ever have to face. I know she won't win, but if you could somehow give her recognition—a personal note, something—it would mean everything to her."

"No problem," Mike said. "I'd be glad to write her a letter on official stationery."

Three weeks later I found a note in my school mailbox: "Call Mike." I phoned immediately. "Your school has the second-place winner," Mike said. My heart stopped. *Sarah? No. Another student.* Any other year, I'd have been pleased beyond words. But I couldn't hide my disappointment. "Will you remember to send the letter?"

"I don't have to," Mike said, gleefully. "The judges felt Sarah's story was so powerful they decided to give a third-place prize. In fact, they were so moved, they pitched in two hundred and fifty dollars for the award. It's a miracle, Lou. I never said a word to them about our conversation."

"Thank you, Mike."

I had to tell Sarah. But I had to savor this miraculous moment and say a prayer of thanks. This is why you teach, a voice seemed to answer. This is how you make a difference. We must never give up. Not on ourselves. Not on others. And certainly not on Sarah.

The Cross in My Pocket

THOMAS GOETZ

One day late in the spring of 1997 I started to ache all over. The pain persisted for a week. Finally I called my doctor, who referred me to a specialist. A CAT scan showed a tumor in my pancreas. Surgery was scheduled, since doctors suspected the mass was malignant.

I was more scared than I had ever been, but I tried to think positively. "I want to use this time before the surgery for us," I told my wife, Nancy. "Let's take a road trip." A couple of days later we climbed aboard our trusty Winnebago and started out.

During our vacation my emotions ran the gamut, and on the way home I continued to feel fearful about the surgery. In North Carolina we stopped for gas. After I filled the tank, a glimmer on the asphalt caught my eye. Lying at my feet was a small aluminum cross. I picked it up and read the words inscribed on the cross-beam—"God Loves You." *This is just what I need right now*, I thought, and put the cross in my pocket. During the rest of the trip, whenever I touched the cross I remembered God would be with me through my ordeal.

When I awoke from the operation I heard my wife saying "benign." Nineteen days later I was discharged. I was so happy to shed the hospital gown for my street clothes. After I dressed, I put my hand in my trouser pocket, and there again I felt the little cross.

At home I found the June issue of *Guideposts*. I opened it and read "Stranger at Union Station." The author, Perry Roll, told about how he had missed a bus and went into a restaurant to wait for the next one. When a woman came in and sat near him, he had an urge to give her the cross—with the inscription "God Loves You"—that he had been carrying in his pocket for years.

The urge persisted, and he obeyed. The woman read the inscription and started to cry. "I have never needed these words more," she said, explaining that her daughter had died a few months earlier and her husband had just left her. Feeling abandoned by everyone—especially God—she had planned to kill herself with a gun she had in her purse . . . until Perry handed her his cross.

Like Perry, I had intended to keep my cross for myself. But not anymore. I will pass it on when the time is right. Sharing God's love with another is what miracles are all about.

The Quiet Miracle of Quilts

DARLENE THACKER

I grew up in the hollers of southern Appalachia, where we lived in a frame schoolhouse built in 1873 on a quarter acre of land. My mother raised four children virtually by herself. My father worked in timber—when he wasn't in jail or chasing women or making moonshine. He often deserted us, but during those hard times Mama was a shining example. Most days she went into the garden to till the soil before daylight with a pickaxlike tool called a mattock. She had the biggest garden, the cleanest house, and the prettiest flowers in the whole holler. And both of us loved singing with all our hearts during services in the tiny Log Pile Church; that was the only social outlet we had.

Mama loved to crochet, and even though she couldn't read a pattern, she could copy the most intricate ones, sometimes using fine #60 sewing-machine thread she had reclaimed from the seams of old clothes. She embroidered pillowcases with rose insets and bartered them for groceries, and she got ten dollars for her quilts. I couldn't believe it when she traded a real nice one for my first

Chihuahua puppy. Even with our limited means, Mama always managed to do something special to cheer us kids up when one of us had a setback.

I never heard her complain about her own hardships, though. Never. Then one day when I was hanging around the house not knowing what to do with myself, I watched Mama from the doorway, careful not to disturb her. She looked for all the world like a figure in a museum painting, sitting there in her chair by the window, bent slightly into the sunlight. Her crochet needle flew faster than I had imagined possible, her fingers moving in a fluid dip-and-pull motion. I was mesmerized. Mama never made a bad stitch.

When I saw her heave a sigh, I strained to see if she was all right.

She's crying! I realized. Mama always made us feel secure, even when Daddy wasn't around. She told us God's angels were watching over us, and reminded us how much we had to be hopeful and thankful for. But who reminded Mama of her blessings when she was feeling defeated? Who comforted her?

In that moment I began to understand what it was that kept Mama strong. Her faith and her quilting were the interwoven constants of her life. *This is where she works out her problems*, I thought, *alone with her prayers and her quilts.*

I went to my room and sat on my bed, thinking

about Mama's life. Through her disappointments, through all her joy, God was an ever-present companion, close by and comforting her while she worked. How many pieces had I seen her start and finish? When she put the final touches on a quilt, the fabric piled in her lap was ready to comfort someone else. I imagined all the folks she had touched and given solace through her needlework, and I was proud. That day I learned the true value of Mama's ten-dollar quilts.

Eventually Mama attracted notice at local quilting contests and became a national prizewinner. She made a quilt for President Dwight D. Eisenhower and corresponded with six First Ladies. But her crowning glory is her final quilt, hand-pieced of tiny five-eighth-inch squares, depicting Jesus and three lambs. It's called "Ninety and Nine," from Jesus's parable of the lost sheep. Thousands of hours went into it, and my sister and I, both quilters ourselves, insisted it was her finest creation.

"I didn't make it," Mama said. "The angel on my shoulder did."

When I think of Mama, I think of her bent over her work in the sunlight, her fingers flying. She is gone from this earth now, but she left masterpieces behind. Her quilts are not simply pieces of beautifully stitched cloth; they inspire and give comfort. They are small miracles of human love. Every time I dip my needle into my quilting, I imagine Mama as the angel on my shoulder. Her example guides me in my life and in my craft, for needlework is the thread that strings our kindred hearts together.

Pride Goeth Before a Water Ticket

ELIZABETH J. SCHMEIDLER

Just weeks before our summer vacation, our doorbell rang at 8:30 in the morning. Puzzled by who could be visiting at such an early hour on the weekend, I peeked out to see a police officer standing on my porch. My heart sank as I thought of the possibility that one of my older sons had been in an accident, since both had already left for work that morning.

I quickly opened the door. Much to my relief, rather than bad news, the officer proceeded to ask me if I knew that I had water running down the street.

"We do?" was my reply. I went on to politely explain to him that we have a sprinkler system that is precisely set so as to conserve water, not waste it, and I asked him if he was sure the water was coming from our lawn. He was not impressed with my fortitude. On the contrary, he asked me to show him some form of ID.

I was just shocked. There he was, standing in my

own home asking me for ID. This was just too much, not to mention that now he would see my weight on my driver's license too.

My youngest son kept saying, "Mom, what'd you do? What'd you do, Mom?"

Emphatically, I answered, "Nothing!"

I tried very hard to remain calm. I knew this was some sort of test, especially when he proceeded to write me up a ticket. *Surely this is just a warning,* I thought. *Surely. Nope. It was a ticket.* Not only was it real, but the officer proceeded to tell me that I would not be given the chance to pay the fine, but rather, I would have to appear in court! As he circled my court date with his pen, my mind slipped into sheer disbelief. Wait a minute, is this some kind of joke? My birthday's coming up; where are the cameras?

Nope. No joke. He was real and so was the ticket. *This can't be happening!* I thought. *I am a law-abiding citizen. I pay my taxes and I am honest! We make our kids obey the laws . . . they're not allowed to drive before they are sixteen, and we don't let them drink alcohol!* My thoughts were spinning! My mind went on and on with our attributes while at the same time I pictured myself standing in line at the courthouse with all the men in the orange suits and handcuffs. I was just mortified.

After dropping my youngest off at his violin practice

that morning, I cried and scolded God, "This is why people get discouraged! All I did was answer the door; that's all. It was just a leaky gasket! I didn't even know the sprinkler system was on! Why did you let this happen?" I figured God already knew what I was thinking, so I might as well say it.

Normally, I am one of those "morning people" who some would like to clobber for being overly positive, but because of many recent disappointments, I guess I was weary of a world where wrong is often called right, and right is perceived as wrong. It wasn't about the ticket. It was the principle. I had always believed and told my children to obey the law and the law would be just. Though I knew this was a small thing in the scheme of life, at that moment it felt huge.

Through my tears, I told God I was sorry I yelled at Him, but as silly as it sounds, and in reality was, I really did feel let down. It just didn't make sense to me. If I had been speeding through a school zone and endangering lives, I would have been given a ticket and fined, but because my sprinkler system leaked, I was going to have to appear in court at 8:00 A.M. the very morning after we returned from vacation.

God, despite my whining and carrying on, had mercy on me when I received notification that my court appearance had been changed to a later date. Though happy with the date change, needless to say, I was still mortified at the idea of appearing in court. I carried on for days at the injustice of it all and even contacted a city commissioner to try and get the ordinance changed.

Meanwhile, our vacation came and went, and though I felt renewed and grateful to God for our safe and wonderful vacation, my heart felt heavy as I climbed the stone steps of the courthouse. The temperature that July day was about 108 degrees, and with every step I took I felt the weight of disappointment, discouragement, and defeat. I had a brief vision of Jesus's journey to Calvary, and shame washed over me. Saying a quick prayer of forgiveness, I pulled open the heavy courthouse door.

As the coolness of the courthouse swept over me, it took my eyes several moments to adjust to the much darker interior of the building. Within moments, I looked up to see a former catechism student of mine running down the stairs. She was crying and ran straight into my arms.

"You came!" she cried. "You came! Did you get the message? I wanted you to be here!"

I had absolutely no idea what she was talking about. I had no idea she had been trying to reach me. The last I had heard, she had been living out of town. I held her, and when she calmed a bit, she explained that she was in court for a family matter involving her custody. She had previously been in foster care and was hoping to get placed permanently with her biological father. The judge had just ruled that it would take another six months before she could live with her dad. Her foster mother had been trying to reach me, but to no avail. I had been out running errands.

A combination of humility, shame, and wonder all washed over me as I realized that, if it weren't for the infamous ticket and then the change in the court date, I wouldn't have been there for this sweet young girl, who had gone through some very hard times. After all, it wasn't as though I ran into her at the grocery store or at Wal-Mart. I never go to the courthouse for anything.

I assured her that God was aware of all things, both great and small, and told her how I came to be there at that moment in time. We laughed together when I told her the story and what a goof I acted like when I got the ticket. Her laughter quickly replaced her tears. We then prayed that the judge would change his mind or that the delay would go quicker than expected. I promised to keep her in my prayers.

After she left, I walked around the nearest corner and wept. This young woman was special to me. When I first met her, I sensed that she was struggling, and I tried very hard to show her extra love and attention. If I hadn't been there at the courthouse that day, I may never have seen her again.

Upon returning home, I received a phone call from the girl's foster mother. The judge had unexpectedly given the girl a month with her father after all. She is, at this writing, happily and permanently living with him.

To this day, I am still humbled at how many times we cannot or do not see God's hand, yet He is there, holding us, changing us, shaping us, protecting us, refining us. Through every storm, through every trial, great or small . . . He is there.

The Story of Daniel

CHRISTINE TROLLINGER

Hospital ministry can be such a blessing, but it can also cause a person to lose their focus on Christ if we allow it to. On one particular hectic Saturday a couple of years ago, I found myself seriously doubting the usefulness of such a ministry.

The morning began with my running behind schedule, as I was really not feeling much up to doing it in the first place. To top it off, I was late getting to the hospital due to accidentally setting the alarm off at church when I unlocked the door. It was my turn as Team Leader to pick up the Eucharist from the church for our team members in the hospital ministry that week. In my hurried frustration, I could not remember the code.

After several tries, I began to worry about how I would ever get to the hospital on time. For the life of me I could not get the alarm to accept my code, and the incessant ringing of the burglar alarm was really starting to make me break out in a sweat.

Struggling to find my code in my purse, I finally located it and discovered I had transposed the numbers.

"Drat!" I wondered to myself, *Will I ever learn this new fangled contraption?* Arriving out of breath and full of apologies to the other members of the ministry team, we quickly set to work. After checking the patient logs the receptionist handed us, we split up the hosts and began our appointed rounds.

While riding the elevator to the first floor of patients, I thought to myself, *I can serve Jesus today and take Him to those who need Him so very much.* I was trying very hard to talk myself into being cheerful and enthusiastic. That thought started working as I came to the first floor, but by the eleventh floor my spirit was beginning to lag once again. Feeling dejected, I began to wonder why we even bothered giving up our time on Saturdays to do hospital ministry. That Saturday was much like the last few we had experienced. We volunteer our time to bring the Eucharist to the hospitalized, and most of the patients are totally disinterested. The usual response was, "No, thanks. I don't care to receive." Some of the patients would even tell you outright they were not happy to be bothered with a visit. That Saturday morning it began to look as if I would have to return most of the hosts to the church again.

As I checked in at the nursing station on the eleventh floor, I was beginning to get the definite feeling that I needed to step back from hospital ministry for a time. It had gotten to be very disheartening to have so many people not interested in receiving. They all seemed to be too busy wanting to see their doctor or involved in phone conversation that I began to feel like the unwanted guest at a wedding reception.

As the nurse handed me back the approved patients list, I found there were only three patients on this last floor to visit, and only two of them could receive the Eucharist. The third patient was marked for a prayer visit only. I had to brace myself mentally for more refusals as I walked toward the first room to meet with a patient named Martha. I was definitely not happy or in a cheerful mood. I worked mightily to paste a smile on my face and appear cheerful, even though I felt like just calling it a day and going home.

As I tapped on the door gently, I prepared to announce myself. But before I could utter a word, this very weak but beautiful voice said; "OH! Come in please! You have brought me my Jesus! I could see His light coming down the hall towards my room."

As I fully entered, I saw a lady who was eagerly anticipating her visit from the Divine Physician. This woman, I would learn later, had come to the hospital for the last time. Martha was in the final stages of her cancer battle, but her soul was at peace as she eagerly awaited her Lord!

Standing in her presence, I felt humbled and quite sure that I was witnessing a little miracle. Martha needed no one to tell her Jesus was present. Her eyes gazed at the Host with what I can only describe as sheer rapture. It was as if the veil of the Tabernacle opened and Christ stepped forth to hold His dying child in His arms Himself. To say the least, I was chagrined at my earlier grumpy thoughts of how useless our ministry was. I left Martha to make the next patient visit with a contrite spirit, and I was full of joy to have been able to bring Christ to one sweet soul that day.

In the moments before I approached the next room, I paused with tears coursing down my cheeks and whispered to Jesus, "I'm sorry for being so grumpy about giving my time to carry You to the sick. Martha has shown me, Lord, how much You care. I know that it's worth every minute of my time. I am a very poor instrument to bring You to the sick and suffering. Please forgive me, Jesus!"

Checking with the next patient's nurse, I found that this patient had a whole room full of visitors. Jim and his family members were very warm and welcoming, and they all wanted to receive Jesus! After leaving Jim and his family still deep in their prayers of thanksgiving for Christ in the Eucharist, I stopped outside the room of my last patient.

Checking with his nurse, I was a bit startled when she replied, "Daniel is probably not worth bothering with, but go on in if you want to." By this time I knew for certain that Christ wanted me to make the effort, even if it would be a waste of time. He had showed me how much He was appreciated by Martha and Jim's family, and I was determined not to disappoint Him again with my poor attitude.

I gently tapped on the door and announced myself to the motionless figure lying in the darkened hospital room. At the sound of my voice, Daniel turned over as best he could. In that instant, I found myself looking into the most beautiful blue eyes I believe I have ever seen—eyes which smiled with the brightness of all heaven, as if to say, "Welcome! How happy I am that you have come to visit me!" Eyes, which mesmerized me with their beauty, even though Daniel, poor creature, was covered with the most awful pustules, which had disfigured his face. I could hardly recognize his nose, and his mouth was full of the most haphazard gapping teeth I'd ever seen. Daniel, it turned out, was profoundly retarded, as well as very physically misshapen. But in my heart of hearts, I knew that Daniel not only recognized Jesus . . . to me he *became* Jesus in this most distressing disguise.

As I prayed at Daniel's bedside, I believed I could hear the angels singing, *"Glory to God in the Highest and to all His creatures on earth!"* Daniel, even though he was mute and physically and mentally challenged, renewed my spirit more than I can say. I came to *bring*

Jesus to the sick and the suffering, but I *found* Jesus that day through the love for Christ in the Eucharist of a dying woman named Martha. Jesus was there in the midst of Jim's family, and in the end, I found Jesus was truly present in the blue eyes of a man named Daniel.

The Great Haylift

BONNIE SILVER

I hadn't been paying attention to the national news that July because it was haying time on our small Michigan farm. My husband, Ron, and I raised a dozen Hereford cattle, and I worried about Ron being stuck out side in the heat when I went to my cashier's job at our local grocery store that Saturday afternoon. As I lay down for a short rest before my shift, I started to pray that Ron wouldn't overdo it. Before I could finish, three words burst into my mind: *hay . . . drought . . . south.* It was the oddest thing. More like a command, really. And with it came such enormous pressure on my body that, for a moment, even breathing became difficult. Finally, I sat up, tears in my eyes. Why was I crying?

I walked into the kitchen. Ron was having a cup of coffee. I asked, "What do the words *hay . . . drought . . . south* mean to you?" He told me there was a terrible drought in the South. Fields were parched, and farmers were losing their cattle because the animals didn't have any hay or feed.

I knew how I'd feel if our cattle were dying. "Ron," I said, "that explains my message." I described the cryptic words and the urgency that had overcome me.

"So what are you going to do about it?" Ron asked.

I had no idea. I didn't know anybody important. I was just a farm wife and a part-time cashier. *God*, I implored, *find someone else to help those farmers.*

But later that day when I was chatting with folks at my checkout counter, I kept thinking, *Hay . . . drought . . . south.* The words wouldn't leave my mind.

At church on Sunday, I reminded God that the drought in the South wasn't really something I could do anything about. Yes, we had some hay to spare, but how could we move it down south? By Monday morning, when the urging just wouldn't go away, I made a few calls to put the matter to rest. I spoke to some other local farmers. Sure, they'd be glad to donate hay, but there was no way they could send it to the ravaged areas. As for our state's ag department, they hadn't organized a thing.

"See, Father," I said, "if they aren't going to do anything, how can I? Please, find someone else."

Hay . . . drought . . . south.

By noon, I did the only thing I could think of. On the highway, I'd often seen trucks from Steelcase, a huge office-furniture manufacturer in Grand Rapids. Maybe they would ship hay. If I made this one call I could be done with it. After all, who'd take me seriously?

I looked up Steelcase's number in the phone book and dialed. Almost immediately, I was connected with a woman in public relations. To my amazement, she gave me the CEO's private number. Before I lost my nerve, I called and reached his secretary.

"What would you like to speak to him about?" she asked. "If I told you, dear," I said, "you'd round-file me as a nut."

Minutes later, the CEO of Steelcase, a company with thousands of employees, called me back. I told my story, concluding by saying, "Michigan farmers want to donate hay to the South, but they can't get it there."

"How many trucks would you need, Mrs. Silver?" he asked.

"Twenty," I said without a pause. *Where did that number come from?*

"Expect a call from Mr. Marlotti. He should be able to help you."

Half an hour later, when Mr. Marlotti did call, telling me that he was instructed to give me whatever I needed, I hooted into the phone. At that moment, I realized this was much bigger than me. All I could do was follow.

OK, God, I prayed, *You win. I'll do what You want, but You have to help me along the way.*

He did. That day I contacted Bill Penn, director of the U.S. Agricultural Stabilization and Conservation Department in Lansing. He promised to send a rep to our house to meet with the Steelcase people and folks from the state ag department so we could coordinate shipments of hay to the South. Meanwhile, someone from Bill's office set up an 800 telephone number to our house. The "Michigan Haylift" was under way.

When the media got hold of the story, broadcasters and newspapers announced the 800 number and all those people ended up calling me.

Twenty-four hours a day the phone in our kitchen rang. We even had an extra line added. People would try to dump hay in our front yard. Reporters interviewed me at the checkout counter at work. Finally, my supervisor suggested I take some time off.

"I want you to devote yourself to the hay project," he said. *Amen*, I thought.

Sometimes, I didn't know how I'd manage. One day, I was sitting in my kitchen when the phone rang. "We've got 500 bales of hay over here in the Thumb." (Michigan is shaped like a mitten, and the eastern peninsula is referred to as the Thumb.)

"Hang on," I replied, checking the map. "We'll get to you." Then I prayed, *God send me someone who can pick up 500 bales of hay, 150 miles away, and get them to the first convoy of semis going south.*

I hadn't even hung up when the other line rang. "I've got an empty truck," a man said. "How can I help?"

"I know just where you're needed!" Things like that kept happening.

On July 24, Bill Penn called from Lansing. "We need you here for a meeting with all the government departments who are involved. I want them to hear from you about what's happening."

I panicked. There was no way I could appear at a meeting in the capital. "I can't," I said. "I can't leave these phones. I can't drive in big cities, and I can't leave the farm."

"You have to be here," Bill insisted. "I'll send a driver to pick you up." How could I argue with that?

When I walked into the conference room in Lansing, I thought I was going to hyperventilate. The table seemed as long as a football field, and around it sat representatives of the state's ag and transportation departments, the governor's office, and the state police. They all looked so official.

"Mrs. Silver," Bill Penn said to me, "would you tell these gentlemen about what you're doing?"

I looked at all those suits, said a quick prayer, and spoke. As clearly as I could, I explained about the thousands of farmers donating hay and people volunteering trucks, and how urgent it was to get the cattle feed to the drought-stricken farmers in the South. I told them that I had cattle and knew how terrible I'd feel if I couldn't feed them. At the end of my speech, a young man from our U.S. senator's office stood up.

"Bonnie," he said, "we've talked to Conrail. You've got as many railcars as you need."

The Lord was working in so many people's lives. The Michigan Haylift was growing by leaps and bounds.

With the railroad involved, we had a more efficient way to ship hay to the South. Drivers picked up hay from farms and delivered them to the sixteen rail sites that were set up. Then volunteers loaded the hay onto railcars for the trip south.

One August night, after I collapsed into bed, Ron asked me how much longer I could keep up my part of the organizing, answering phones, talking to reporters, giving out information.

"Until the job's finished," I said.

"When will that be?"

"I don't know," I answered wearily.

In mid-August, I went to Grand Rapids to see first-hand what was going on. High-school football teams, youth-corps volunteers, prisoners on work detail, all kinds of people were taking the hay from trucks and putting it into railcars. It was brutal work, especially in the heat, but no one slowed down. Good thing McDonald's, Burger King, and Pepsi donated massive amounts of food and beverages to keep everyone going.

We started getting reports from grateful farmers down south whose cattle were getting fed again. We were delivering hay into seven states—over 10.5 million pounds—and not one dollar had exchanged hands. All the labor, fuel, transportation, and feed were donated.

Then one morning in September, a TV reporter came to do an update on the story. I tried to answer her questions, but my words just wouldn't come out right. "Excuse me," I said, "you'll have to talk to my husband."

After the TV crew left, I smiled at Ron. "I guess it's time."

"What's time?" he asked.

"You wondered how I'd know when I was finished. Well, all these months, God's given me the strength to do things I would've never been able to do on my own. But today I can't. I think that's His way of telling me I'm finished."

Drought conditions eased and the project did wind down after that. Our phones stopped ringing; we took out the extra line; people stopped bringing hay to our farm; and I returned to my job at the grocery store. Only one blessing remained, and that was meeting some of the folks who'd been on the receiving end.

On a rainy Thanksgiving weekend—how fitting that it rained—we joined hundreds of others under a big tent outside Greenville, South Carolina. A choir sang, a minister led us in prayer, and a proclamation from the governor was read. "Thank you, Bonnie," people said. "We're so grateful for what you did."

The real thanks belonged to the Lord, for whom I was only a reluctant servant. But He gives us what we need to do His will. That's what I learned. He gave me willingness when I was unwilling, words when I was tongue-tied, stamina when I was weak. How else would a farm wife and part-time cashier ever have been able to help start the Great Michigan Haylift?

Editor's Note: Since this story happened in 1987, Bonnie and Ron have turned part of their acreage into a wildlife preserve. Their love of farming and animals is as strong as ever—as is their belief in the difference one person plus God can make.

Hayden's Miracle

AIMEE PERRINE

Hayden has the curly golden hair of an angel. He is three years old and has the predictability of a tornado in his capacity to love people as well as destroy property. Hayden was blessed with a miracle just before his third birthday this past summer. It's hard to believe anyone could need a miracle quite so soon in their young life, but he did. Maybe I needed it more.

He was born at home and was perfect in every way until his fourteenth day when he turned black and stopped breathing in my arms while my husband was at a wedding an hour away. Alone and shrieking in terror I managed to call 911. The woman who answered was able to calm me down enough to perform CPR. I was never able to thank her in all the drama, but because she was able to stop my shrieking, Hayden never suffered brain damage and I am eternally grateful.

After loads of excruciating testing, the doctors figured out he had four kidneys and many ureters. Urine was refluxing from his bladder back up into his kidneys causing life-threatening damage. It wasn't likely, but they hoped he might grow out of it. As it turned out, he didn't. Postsurgical follow-up discovered that bladder surgery had only helped one side. During recovery his pain was so intense that his crying and writhing in agony created a hernia. As the months passed, it would appear and disappear until suddenly one night after his bath he began screaming and vomiting and had to be rushed in for surgery. Unfortunately this was only a month before his second scheduled surgery. Follow-up testing after his third surgery indicated the problem still wasn't fixed. We would need to come back in May to decide when and what the next surgery would be.

Sunday afternoon, the weekend before Hayden's Monday morning May appointment, my husband and I met a woman during lunch at a seminar. Each of us at our table of four was chatting a little bit about what we do, getting to know each other. Across the table from me sat a woman named Debra. She told us she was a nurse, but that the most amazing thing she did to help her patients she couldn't even tell them about. We all stopped eating suddenly, looked up from our plates expectantly, curiosity piqued, as she told us how she is part of a World Wide Healing Prayer Circle. She explained how a few nights a week at a specific time she and thousands of other people pray for someone together.

My eyes welled up as I asked her what a person had

to do to be on the list. Through a flood of tears I described Hayden's situation, how he had endured more pain and torture in the two small years that he had been alive than 98 percent of grownups would *ever* experience. Suddenly she stood up, pulled her phone out of her white purse, and walked away. She came back a few minutes later grinning widely, blue eyes sparkling, and announced it was all set up! That was Sunday at lunchtime. By 3:00 Monday, the very next day, Hayden did not need surgery anymore.

We held our breath as Hayden's doctor slid his fresh new ultrasound pictures up onto the light box next to the ones from a few months before. He went back and forth between the two sets of pictures studying for quite a while and then turned to us. "He looks great," the doctor announced! "Does he need surgery?" we asked. "No, he has made a complete recovery!"

Debra was the first person I called, as you can imagine, but God was the first One we thanked. As I type this now, the whole thing makes me cry all over again from a deep ache of gratitude that wells up from my soul. It's the kind of gratitude that helps me not care so much about the hole Hayden drilled in the playroom wall today with my giant flamingo pen, or the fact that he unceremoniously stuck his bum into his Easter basket this morning and became wedged as the bottom of the basket burst out and he wet his pants on the playroom floor, or about the brand-new block of cheese he snuck out of the refrigerator and hid in the couch that we only found because of the smell. Thank God for little boys.

Last-Minute Miracle

KREGG GRIPPO

I don't have time for this," I muttered to myself, pulling my truck into the overgrown lot on the outskirts of town. I own a small construction company in upstate New York. A friend of a friend had asked if I'd do him a favor. An elderly woman had been burned out of her home.

"She's been living in a little shack out there since May," he said. "Christmas is coming. I thought maybe you could help her out."

I eyeballed the property. *Help her out how?* There was a rickety old garden shed and the charred remains of a modest house far beyond repair. *What am I supposed to do—build her a new house?* Out of the question. I had a business to run. And this time of year was the worst.

Just then the shed door opened, and an elderly woman wearing a bright red scarf and wrapped in a too-light coat came out. Instead of warm boots, she wore old sneakers.

"Mrs. Turek," I said, "I'm Kregg Grippo."

"Grippo?" She cocked her head. "Are you related to Elizabeth Grippo?"

"That's my aunt. Don't tell me you know her."

"Long ago," she said. "We were schoolmates. I taught her to speak English."

When Aunt Elizabeth arrived in this country in 1920, she spoke only her native Italian. It must have been tough learning a whole new language. I moved closer.

"How did your house burn down?" I asked.

Mrs. Turek lowered her eyes. "A log rolled out of the fireplace. I couldn't put the flames out. By the time the fire department arrived, it was too late. The house was gone. I should have left that night. But I couldn't. I've been here almost sixty years. This is my home."

The house had been so small it must have gone up in minutes.

"Where have you been staying?"

She led me to the shed and two cats slipped out. *Oh my*, I thought. The musky smell of cats and old wood wafted up. I followed her inside. The dim light showed a space about the size of a walk-in closet. Pots and pans were scattered on the floor. In the center was an old cot covered in afghans. Particle-board walls were all that separated her from the cold.

I spun around and walked outside. *She should not be staying here*, I thought. That friend of mine. He must have known I couldn't leave Mrs. Turek like this. But I couldn't build a house by myself. I needed a crew. It was almost Christmas. *Who had time? Couldn't she just move to a shelter?*

Suddenly an old saying of my grandmother's—Aunt Elizabeth's mother—came to mind, clear as a church bell: "If it's to be, it's up to me."

"Don't worry, I'll take care of everything," I heard myself tell Mrs. Turek. I loped toward my truck. As I climbed into the cab, I blurted out, "You'll have a new house by Christmas."

Am I crazy? Even if I could lean on a few men, where would I find the materials? My eyes fell on the Bible I keep on the passenger seat in the truck. I thought again of my grandmother's words. *If it's to be, Lord,* I prayed, *it's up to me.*

I called everyone I knew in construction—my crew, suppliers, even a competitor or two. "I need your help," I told them. I called my customers, told them I had an emergency and asked for extensions. Within days, fifteen men arrived in Mrs. Turek's yard, ready to work. We started pounding nails and raising beams. We'd agreed to donate our time, but I didn't know how long we could afford to continue. "Somehow, we're going to make this happen," I said. But even a small house is a big project once you start building.

Word spread. The next morning twenty showed up, then thirty, then a local TV film crew. Mrs. Turek's story ran on the evening news. That night my phone lit up. "Kregg," said a man who explained he was an electrical contractor, "what can I do to help?"

"Saw you on TV," another caller—a plumbing contractor— said, "Anything you need, you got it."

I got calls from roofing companies, heating supply companies, carpet suppliers. A car dealer offered Mrs. Turek use of an RV free of charge until her new house was completed.

The frame went up. We laid out the rooms. Mrs. Turek threw that old scarf over her head, pulled up a lawn chair, and watched her new house go up, like she was watching a movie.

We finished on Christmas Eve. A cozy tan ranch with black shutters. Shiny new appliances adorned the kitchen, and new furniture filled the house. The roofing company guys even chipped in for Christmas presents.

Mrs. Turek stared in disbelief. "It's my little dollhouse," she said, her eyes teary. A few of those tough guys in my crew teared up too, including yours truly.

I walked down the driveway to my pickup. I turned and looked at the house, now all lit up for the holiday. I thought of Aunt Elizabeth and of my grandmother's words again. When there was something you knew God wanted you to do, you took the first step—and you could trust Him with the rest. It was the smallest home I'd ever built, but it gave me the biggest feeling I'd ever had.

Chapter 5

Little Taps of Love from Heaven

God, your ways are holy. No god is as great as our God.
You are the God who does miracles; you have shown people
your power. (Psalm 77:13–14, NCV)

We usually expect God to arrive with claps of thunder and lightning bolts, don't we? And yet, much more often He arrives on the gossamer wings of butterflies, in the shy smile of a tiny child, or in the quiet glow of a golden sunset. And He touches our lives with reflections of His grace in small and mighty ways, if we are astute enough to recognize Him when He comes. He gives us little taps of His love from heaven.

"Go Home, Now!"

VICKI P. GRAHAM

I was a reporter for the nation's oldest newspaper still in publication. The *Virginia Gazette* faithfully fired up the presses once a week and printed a unique blend of historical news and current news, often scooping the bigger and newer daily newspapers out of nearby Newport News, Virginia.

Colonial Williamsburg was one of my beats. CW, as the locals called it, was a living village that recreated life as it was when the USA first began. Costumed workers plied their trades as blacksmiths, tavern employees, silversmiths, and other occupations common to the eighteenth century. The oldest college in America was situated on the grounds of CW. The College of William and Mary, established by Thomas Jefferson and designed by Christopher Wren, the famous architect, was steeped in tradition and the lifestyle of the Revolutionary War era.

Our newspaper was as traditional as William and Mary, and one of the favorite traditions that the staff diligently kept was Friday night happy hour. We would meet at the Greenleaf Café, a bistro-type bar and grill that featured Greek cuisine, that was located on the edge of the campus, and everyone who was anyone would gather to chat and celebrate the end of the workweek.

One such Friday at least fifteen or twenty of us, from pressmen to typesetters to reporters and editors were seated at a huge wooden table. The Greenleaf still had its original furniture, at least two hundred years old. We were especially convivial because of a very rare snow that was covering the grounds of CW and Virginia. We seemed to be laughing more than usual, and the camaraderie was grand.

Suddenly, right in the middle of a huge laugh, I clearly heard a voice tell me "Go home, now!"

I turned to my husband and said, "We have to go home, now." He saw the look on my face and immediately rose to leave.

Our house was nine miles from Williamsburg, and we faced a huge blizzard. We fought the elements while we reassured each other that our children were safe. Our daughter was fifteen, plenty old enough to baby-sit our five-year-old son; so we knew they were okay. Why did a voice tell me we should go home immediately?

Finally we made it home. As we pulled into our driveway, our daughter's friend came running through the snow.

"Thank God, you're home!" she shouted. "I came to find you. Nik has just been hit by a car. An ambulance is on the way."

We ran after her to where our road curved just as the ambulance blasted past us. There was our precious son lying in the ditch, unconscious. I climbed in the ambulance while Nik was being loaded, and my husband prepared to follow us back to town to the hospital. Again we faced the elements of this rare blizzard as the ambulance sped through the night.

Thankfully, Nik regained consciousness and required only a few stitches to his head, but the doctor wanted him admitted and watched through the night. As we sat in his room thanking God for His mercy, we rehashed the events of the past few hours. At the same time we both came to the same conclusion.

While we sat in the Greenleaf Café and the word came to me to go home *now*, it was still at least twenty minutes before Nik was hit by the car. We were on the road to our house *before* the accident happened. What providence was good enough to let us know we needed to be there to support him before he was hit and thrown out the car? It had to be a miracle from our merciful God!

My New Life

JOAN GATTUSO

Ginna Bell Bragg, my best friend ever since high school, called me from California. "Joan, I'm getting married!"

Married—the word made me shudder. Still, I congratulated her. And I meant it. I was happy for her; it was my own situation that seemed impossible.

Ginna went off to California after high school, but I married in 1979 and settled down in my hometown of Akron, Ohio. Bill was older, a take-charge type; to me that meant security. Bill wore the pants in our family. He was strict about how money was spent, insisting on keeping our funds separate and never letting me forget he was the one who earned more. Soon I discovered my husband wanted to control more than the purse strings. He wanted to control every aspect of my life. He was highly critical, and we argued constantly. At first I tried to shrug off his sharp words. *If I just love him enough our marriage will improve*, I told myself. And that's what I asked God for every day—more love for my husband and a healed relationship.

But Bill's angry words became pushes and shoves. I never knew what would set him off. *What am I doing wrong?* I asked God. I began to wonder if He was hearing me at all. He could fix anything; why wasn't He fixing my marriage?

Now Ginna wanted me to fly out to California for her wedding. But Bill would never agree to let me go. "Oh, Ginna, I'd love to come. I just don't know . . . "

"Joan, don't let me down. You know I'd be there for you, no matter what."

We had shared every secret during our awkward teenage years. They were more awkward for me than for Ginna. She was popular and outgoing. I was quiet and reserved. But Ginna didn't care. She said our personalities complemented each other and she knew she could trust me. Her enthusiasm and daring were catching, and I found myself doing things with her that I never would have done alone. We were a great team.

That didn't change after we became adults. Before my marriage, while in college, I noticed the artwork in the campus chapel needed to be restored, but I hesitated to approach the director. As usual, I called Ginna for advice. She reminded me how I had encouraged her to follow her dream and go back to art school. She told me it was my turn to muster my courage and talk to the director. I did, and ended up in charge of the two-year restoration.

I knew Ginna would always be there for me. And I needed her more than ever. "Okay, Ginna, I'll be there." It was the boldest decision I had made for myself since I got married.

I summoned all the confidence I had and told Bill my plans. I think he was too shocked to react.

"It's just for the weekend," I said. But inside I had decided something else. Maybe I would stay away longer than that. Maybe forever.

My job at a small church outside Cleveland was the one thing Bill allowed me to do on my own. He criticized my connection to the church, but he didn't try to stop me from going.

I started putting a little cash aside, slipping it into an old purse. I scrimped and saved, cutting corners where Bill wouldn't notice. The whole time I kept asking God to change my situation, to work a miracle.

The night before I was to fly to California, I went to add a slip to my suitcase. I was about to snap the buckle closed when I sensed Bill behind me. I could tell by his breathing and his terrible energy that something had set him off. I couldn't turn around. I didn't want to see his face.

Bill snatched my suitcase and flung it across the room. Clothes flew everywhere. Terrified, I faced him. He'd found the money.

"What's going on?" he demanded.

He grabbed me and shoved me down on the bed. His face, contorted with anger, pushed close to mine. *He's going to kill me.*

He screamed threats at me. His hands tightened around my neck. I tried to push him off me. I clutched at his hands to loosen his grip. It was no use. I was helpless. Finally, hardly able to form the prayer in my mind, I begged, *God, please . . .*

An answer washed over me: Only love is real. Only perfect love exists.

I had read those words in a book about miracles and had repeated them during my meditations, but never fully understood their meaning. What was God trying to tell me? The words filled my mind. Desperate, I concentrated on them and not on what was happening to me.

Then, strangely, I felt a powerful shift of energy in the room. My husband suddenly let go. His hands dropped to his sides. He got off the bed and slowly backed away. At the door he turned and, without a word, left the room.

All night I stayed on the bed, praying and crying, asking God for strength. I had to get out of the house. But how? I was too afraid even to leave the room.

By morning, though, I realized I had to act or I might never get another chance. I repacked my suitcase. *God, please walk with me.* I moved out of the bedroom and out of the house. My husband didn't follow.

That weekend in California was the balm I needed. When we got some time alone, I finally told Ginna my secret.

"Don't go back," she said.

"But how will I get along?"

"You're stronger than you think," Ginna said. "Remember when you took on that chapel restoration?"

"I didn't think I could handle it at first . . . "

"But you found the strength to do it. You've got to do the same thing now," she urged. "You have to get out of this dangerous situation."

I nodded. I knew she was right.

Ginna hugged me tight. "You can do anything you set your mind to, with God's help," she said.

I returned to Ohio, rented a small apartment, got counseling, and attended workshops and spiritual retreats. Sometimes when I talked about what had happened, my tears fell uncontrollably. My entire body shook. Hateful, fearful thoughts ripped through me. *Why had I stayed for so long? Why had I allowed anyone to treat me that way?* Not only was I angry at my ex-husband, I was angry at myself. I knew I would remain trapped by that bad relationship until I took the crucial step: I had to forgive—my ex-husband and myself. I wasn't sure I could do it, but I remembered what Ginna had said, "You can do anything you set your mind to, with God's help."

Daily I asked God for the strength to forgive. Early one morning I picked up a legal pad. At the top of the page I wrote, "I forgive everybody. I forgive myself. I'm free. I'm free."

Underneath, I wrote my ex-husband's name, and as fast as I could, a list of the many things I needed to forgive him for. "I forgive you for hurting me. I forgive you for the names you called me. I forgive you for deriding my job. I forgive you for the fear you instilled in me . . . . " In fifteen minutes I filled three pages. Then I set a lit match to them and flung them in the fireplace. As my painful memories flared up and disintegrated into ashes, I felt the stirrings of the relief I so craved. I sat quietly in prayer. Again I recalled: *Only love is real. Only perfect love exists.* And for the first time the meaning of those words was crystal clear: God in His perfect love will exist for all eternity. Anything outside of that—anger, hatred, fear—is impermanent. It cannot survive in the face of God's perfect, abiding love.

My list making became a discipline. Three mornings a week I scribbled on my notepad, then burned the hateful memories, giving up anger and letting love in. Eventually the lists became harder to write. I could no longer remember vividly the terrible acts committed by my ex-husband. Slowly forgiveness came, like a gentle tide, quenching the flames of my anger, sadness, and hurt. I had confronted each feeling, each memory, then let it go. A different me emerged. A strong, vibrant, happy me. Just like the person Ginna had always believed in and had insisted God wanted me to be.

I had asked God to change my situation. He had changed me, with His perfect, purifying love.

The Sustaining Power

GREGORY DEIBERT

Being a twenty-four-hour tow-truck owner/operator is difficult at best. Add to that a pregnant wife, a three-year-old daughter, and a suburban home that demands too much money, and an all too common picture is created. Life becomes a constant exercise in time-stretching. Your family needs you, your business needs you, your church needs you, and so on, or so it seems, infinitely. The eighteen-hour workdays pile up until you realize that you've lost control of your life.

I remember looking forward to Sunday worship service because it was the only time I could turn off my beeper. With deadly persistence, this pattern continued with all the appearance of worldly success, while in reality I was spiritually dying with my family falling apart. I knew it! I could feel my love for Jesus slipping away. I recognized the increase in strife at home. I wasn't a new Christian easily confused by these things; I simply felt powerless to stop them.

"For what shall it profit a man, if he shall gain the whole world, and lose his own soul?" (Mark 8:36, KJV)

I had to have a radical change. I was sure I needed it soon. Without some form of special help from the Lord Jesus, I would drown in a sea of stress.

About two o'clock one morning in July 1979, I pulled up in front of my friend's apartment with my 1970 one-ton wrecker. He wasn't surprised to see me. Jim and I often got together at late hours to study or pray. Lately I hadn't shown up as often. His apartment was small, and the high humidity of a midsummer night only emphasized the close quarters of his kitchen. "Lord Jesus," I prayed, "I'm not willing to continue my life the way it is, take it all and bless it or burn it."

I left my house the next morning after my usual two-and-a-half hours' sleep. I was unhappy with myself, angry with my customers, and ready to do whatever was necessary to make another dollar. The day was too short, as always, and I was standing in the yard of our shop trying to start one car after just towing in two. I heard Bob, the mechanic, yell something. He was telling me that the carburetor I was trying to prime with gasoline was still hot from his earlier efforts. I was too busy to listen. I ordered the man in the car to turn the key.

The explosion that followed tore the skin from my left hand and arm. The gasoline I held was thrown onto my chest and legs, then burst into flame. I felt and saw my body being consumed by fire. The effort to extinguish the burning mixture of clothes, gasoline, and my flesh, took all of my strength. Paralyzed in both legs and my left arm, I fought fear and pain to reach a nearby pickup truck. Wes, my helper, got me to a hospital by breaking every speed and traffic law in the books. It wasn't fast enough. I was dying from a heavy loss of fluid coupled with massive blood loss and shock.

After the doctor examined me in the emergency room, I heard him say, "There's nothing I can do for him."

I asked him, "Am I dying?"

He turned and left me without answering. All this took place as though in a nightmare, with reality only a hazy mist in front of me. I felt as if I could let go of the fiery torment of pain and slip comfortably into death merely by choosing to do so. I turned to Wes, who by now was praying desperately, and said, "Whatever the price, I want to live."

God recognized the decision. I cannot explain this, for I do not fully understand, but I know it was what He wanted from me. I felt alertness intensify through every avenue of my body as His Spirit covered me. My mind and attention were focused on spiritual matters, and I began witnessing about the power of God to the medical attendants.

The horror of pain was still upon me, and I screamed, but Wes and the nurses watched me as, between outbursts of pain, I smiled and almost laughed at the realization of God's presence.

At this point, orders were given to transfer me to St. Agnes Burn Center in Philadelphia for emergency treatment. I was injected with high doses of painkiller about three hours after the accident and told that I would soon be asleep. Not only did I not sleep then, but the next twenty-four hours found me alert and attentive despite further injections. Attempts to put me to sleep failed. The dosages and types of drugs given me are recorded on the medical charts. I cannot physically explain their ineffectiveness; God simply wanted me awake.

Questions churned in my mind. *Would I keep my arm? Have any use of my hand? How could my business operate without me? Where were my wife and daughter? How would Cheryl react to the strain, being four months pregnant? Would she still love a man who was permanently disabled?*

We call Him Lord. Every day of our lives we say Lord this or Lord that, yet I am convinced, we do so without a full realization of the power of His Lordship. For as panic began to sweep in a wave of anxiety over me, I heard Him say, "I AM LORD," as He seized control of my emotions and calmed them as easily and as completely as He spoke to the waves of the Sea of Galilee two thousand years ago. He was establishing His authority over me. I am fully aware of our God-given freedom of will; still, when we turn our lives over to Him, I discovered, He reserves the right to intervene and direct our thoughts, emotions, our very motivations.

If space permitted, I would tell of the miracles that allowed me to keep my arm, redevelop use of my hand, and struggle to walk again. The long weeks of hospitalization, skin grafting, blood transfusions and much more had me walking a mental and spiritual tightrope. God plainly allowed me to heal, the delicate chemistry of life restored at amazing speed. But what of the other things, the things I could not control?

My business had stopped, my major contract had been broken, and my wife was showing signs of stress that her smiling conversation did not conceal, Still, I knew that God was real and was working in our lives with obvious power.

I had been home for two weeks. The scars didn't bother me; they bothered my wife less. Life was good. We had found an appreciation for each other as never before. I was lying in bed considering all this when suddenly my six-month-pregnant wife stood in the doorway of our room. "I'm in labor!" she said.

Later, the doctor's voice penetrated: "Mr. Deibert, we are doing this for your wife; the water is gone and there is too great a chance of infection. Unfortunately, the child will probably not live through the delivery."

A nameless baby boy—one pound, fifteen ounces—was born at Jefferson Hospital in Philadelphia. Nameless because the doctors involved had cautioned the father about psychological and emotional risks to the mother in giving a name to a dying infant.

I remembered how Joshua had led the people dry-shod across the Jordan River. I remembered how God wanted him to place great stones at that location as a reminder of the mighty miracle. I stared at my scarred body and the hand that shouldn't be there. Then I spoke with quiet authority to a nearby nurse. "Give him my name." Gregory Wallace Deibert Jr. would not die nameless. In fact, he would not die! The Holy Spirit of the God of Joshua had flooded me with faith and told me so.

His lungs were not developed. I was assured that, even given the slim chance of life, he would be physically, possibly mentally, impaired. He was too small to stand the strain of the respirator that slammed down on his chest. Everything was wrong, yet the peace that Cheryl and I had through a two-month process of intensive care was purely of God.

During those two months I took milk from home to the hospital three times a day. The seventy-mile round trip was especially hard at 3:00 A.M., but never once did I become ill or unable to function, despite having just had three major skin grafts and losing forty pounds. The sustaining power of God is a limitless source of untapped energy. He can literally carry you when your mind and body fail.

Today I sit on the living room sofa and watch nine-month-old Gregory Jr. play in his walker. His completely normal and healthy body and mind are testimony of the love of God. I am composing a new song about the Lord to play on my guitar. My four-year-old daughter, Jessica, is sitting next to me trying to help. Cheryl is in the kitchen preparing dinner. I'm sure she's wondering, as she glances my way, why my eyes fill with tears as I smile.

Right On Time

VICKI P. GRAHAM

My husband and I were working for a small oil drilling company selling partial ownerships in our projects. We were earning a fairly nice living through our commissions when the oil bust of 1985 hit us and our company had to close its doors. We were left almost penniless. We had only enough money to pay part of our rent while we looked for other employment. But we lacked four hundred dollars to make the complete payment.

Our landlord would grant us no mercy. He told us we must have the entire payment to him by the next day or else we needed to vacate the property. What could we do to raise four hundred more dollars by the next day?

Our twelve-year-old son joined us in fervent prayer for the money, and the prayer chain of our home church interceded for us. But we couldn't think of a way to prevent our eviction. We didn't even have anything we could sell to raise the money in time.

Many years before the oil bust we owned a home in another state where we invited a friend who was down and out to live with us until she could get on her feet. At one point she was so desperate that she asked to borrow four hundred dollars. We gave her the money, even though she told us she didn't know when she could pay it back.

We had long since lost touch with Molly, and we knew we'd never see the return of our loan. But that was okay because we loved her like a daughter. When you loan money to a friend, you're not supposed to expect a return.

On the morning our payment was due we spent the hours praising the Lord and leaving our financial problems at the cross. Our prayers were interrupted by the clang of the mailbox when the postman made his rounds. My husband went outside to retrieve the mail.

When I heard his scream of joy, I hurried to the door to see what he'd found. He was standing by the mailbox with tears streaming down his face and flapping a piece of paper in my face.

The piece of paper? A check from Molly for four hundred dollars, years later . . . but right on time for us! Is God's mercy exactly on time or what?

When I Stumble

VIKKI DENISI HANSON AS TOLD TO
BONNIE COMPTON HANSON

O H, WHAT a beautiful day!" That's what I wanted
to shout as my young son and I hurried out the
front door one busy fall morning.

I glanced at my watch: eight o'clock. Plenty of time
for an invigorating walk to work in the fresh autumn
air. Although it was already late November, the sky was
bright and cloudless. All the better to show off the
brand-new magenta jumper I had just bought for work.
Yes, I know that magenta is a rather bright color for
work. But I'm a preschool teacher, and "bright" is
exactly what my students love—the wilder, the better!

I guess I've always loved teaching. Especially little
ones. I love to read stories to them, introduce them to
the alphabet and numbers, sing with them, see the
world through their eyes. In fact, I get as excited about
new projects as they do.

So, of course, I hate to miss a single day of work.
Besides, little ones need the security of being around the

same adults each day, as much as possible. It's as hard on them when a teacher is out sick as it is on the teacher!

That's why I felt so discouraged earlier this fall when I seemed to be developing some health problems. I had even fainted one day in October. Grim memories of childhood illnesses haunted me. I always felt so ashamed when I was sick—as though it was all my fault.

So I'd been checking in regularly with my doctor. Things seemed to be under control now, and that was just fine with me. I needed all the energy and creativity I could muster to stay ahead of a roomful of wiggly, giggly four-year-olds. Not to mention my own lively son at home! And I also needed plenty of energy to get ready for Thanksgiving, which was coming up quickly. I knew the added stress could take its toll.

I suddenly felt a little lightheaded, just as I had for a few moments while getting dressed earlier that morning. But I took a deep breath, and the feeling passed. Please, dear God, let me be all right today.

Out on the sidewalk, my son, Daniel, and I turned back to wave to our new home. How I loved living here! We luxuriated in being able to spread out in a roomy house after years in a cramped apartment. Best of all, we now lived close enough for both Daniel and me to walk to our schools.

The last couple of years he had gone to preschool

with me. But now, as a very "grown-up" kindergartner, Daniel attended an elementary school just a couple of blocks away, which worked out perfectly.

Neighborhood kids were his school pals, a friend of mine from church watched him after class, and my mom had been the school's office manager for years. Everyone knew my mom, and Daniel was thrilled to be able to see her every day.

The nearby preschool where I taught was located in the church I had attended most of my life. It was also where Jay and I were married. This special place was where I first learned about God's protection and care of those who love Him. How He sent an angel to protect Daniel in the lions' den and another one to rescue Peter from prison. Why, perhaps this very moment there were angels surrounding Daniel and me to keep us safe as we set off to school!

"There's your school, Daniel!" I said as we rounded the corner. The streets and sidewalks around us were jammed as usual, with parents dropping off carload after carload of excited children. "Good-bye! Have a great day. Say hi to Grandma for me. And think about what you'd like to eat for Thanksgiving!"

As Daniel rushed off to meet his classmates, I shifted the weight of my bags and headed for my own school. High overhead I could see some migrating geese. The yards around me were bright with mums and gold and crimson leaves. The laughter of children filled the air.

As the morning traffic whizzed past me, I began planning for my own school day ahead. The children always loved making handprint "turkeys," so that would be one of our fun projects. We were also going to make Pilgrim hats for our classroom's Thanksgiving celebration later in the week. And thanks to some of our parent volunteers, we were planning to have a complete Thanksgiving dinner at school.

Then, of course, there were my own holiday plans to make. This year, to celebrate our first Thanksgiving in our new home, we had invited a houseful of friends, relatives, and coworkers.

I was thrilled, of course. But apprehensive as well. My mother and mother-in-law would both help cook. But this was my first time hosting a big family holiday. There were all those exhausting details to take care of, like finding enough silverware and plates—plus places for everyone to sit without falling on top of each other. And, of course, I'd have to clean the entire house from top to bottom!

Indeed, just before my husband, Jay, kissed me and left for his own job that morning, I reminded him that we needed to run to the supermarket that evening to get our turkey. I'd finally saved up enough register receipts to get one for free! Already my mind was running through a shopping list of other absolute necessities: pies, yams, gravy, string beans, corn. Plus, of course, cranberries, salad, dressing—the whole works!

With my head full of plans, I stepped off the curb to cross the street. The next thing I knew, I was sprawled in the middle of the street, barely able to lift my head off the ground.

What in the world had happened? Obviously I'd had a very bad fall. But, why? Did I slip on something? Step off the curb wrong? Turn my ankle? Or had I fainted again?

As soon as I could sit up, I checked myself for damage. The contents of my purse, schoolbag, and lunchbox were scattered everywhere. But, amazingly, I had suffered no cuts, no broken bones, no bruises, no swollen ankles. Indeed, no pain of any kind. Just a black stain on one shoulder of my new jumper and a huge hole in my pantyhose.

Suddenly I remembered that I was sitting right in the middle of a very busy street. Terrified, I looked around for oncoming cars. But, amazingly, the street— so crowded just moments before—was now completely empty. As though I were out in the middle of a vast desert. Or a sanctuary.

And then I realized something else. I wasn't alone. A strange woman was right there—to one side and sort of behind me—holding me tight. Because I was still confused and my hair had fallen down over my face, I couldn't see the woman very well. But I did notice that her hair was dark like mine. And she seemed to be dressed in gleaming white.

"Are you all right, honey?" she asked, her voice full of gentle concern.

"Y-yes. Uh, of course, I'm fine."

I was so embarrassed! What if she were the mother of one of my students? Or even one of the new teachers at Daniel's school! If so, she'd probably tell my mom all about it, and I'd never hear the end of it. Mom had always been protective of me, and she had been really worried about my health this fall. In fact, she'd been insisting that I let her drive me to school each morning. I'm the one who kept protesting, "But walking's so healthy!"

"Now you're sure?" the woman in white repeated.

I nodded. "Yes, but thanks again. I really appreciate your help."

Forcing a laugh, I pulled away and started snatching up all my scattered belongings. If this woman had seen me fall, maybe other people had too. Tumbles really aren't dignified for a schoolteacher, and I certainly didn't want to set anyone's tongue to wagging.

Collecting my bags, I insisted, "I'll be just fine, honest." As the woman helped me get up, I reached out to shake my good Samaritan's hand and say good-bye. But there was no one there.

In fact, there was no one but me in the street, on the sidewalk, in the general vicinity.

Everything was as quiet as if someone had turned off all the sound—as if even time itself had stopped. Or as if God had built an invisible, soundproof wall all around me. Then, just like that, all the noises rushed back. Parents, children, and cars whizzed by again. I brushed myself off, reorganized my belongings, and straightened up my clothes. Then I walked on to school and my normal workday world, just as if nothing had happened.

But, of course, something had happened. I had a big stain on my shoulder and torn pantyhose to remind me of that. Along with the still-felt touch of those strong but gentle arms. Whoever's arms they were.

To this day, I still don't know if my mysterious comforter that morning was just another woman who happened to be passing by—a neighbor, a mother who had already delivered her child to school, or one of the school staff.

Or if she was a special divine being God had sent to help me, just as I had asked Him to, by protecting me from injuring myself in that fall. And from being hit by a speeding car. Just as He long ago sent His angels to protect Daniel and Peter.

Those arms had been so comforting, so blessing, so warm . . . as comforting as those of an angel. So full of God's love, strength, and compassion. I do know that His Word promises, "He will command his angels concerning you to guard you in all your ways; they will lift you up in their hands" (Psalm 91:11–12, NIV). And I believe that promise with all my heart.

Amazingly, although every accident near the school was normally reported to the school office, no one ever reported mine. Nobody told my mom or called me up at work or home afterward to check on me.

Maybe I'll never know the identity of my rescuer. But whoever it was God sent, I'm still very thankful to Him for His help both right then and in the busy days that followed. Not that our holiday turned out absolutely perfect: my husband got the flu, the turkey was hard to carve, and the yams were scorched. But even so, everyone who came said it was their best Thanksgiving ever. I know it was for me. I'm still giving thanks!

The Changed Heart

MARY ANN KELLY

Many timely and untimely events have shaped the life of my husband of twenty-seven years. This is true of all people, I suppose, but God worked a miracle in our lives *upon belief*.

Miracles, in my mind, are beyond belief, something supernatural, God-orchestrated, but this miracle occurred fifteen years after I began to ask for it.

Upon moving to Georgia in the late 1980s, we made a commitment to worship God together after a long hiatus and many moves in the military.

After settling into fellowship in a small congregation, we both became active as the leaders of a small group. My husband dutifully led meetings and implemented many of the ideas I suggested. Not long after being pushed and prodded into this service, his enthusiasm began to ebb. I encouraged him and even tried to shame him into continuing his efforts "for the good of the church," until he curtly asked, "Now, why am I doing this? Is my time up yet?"

Of course, I was hurt that he didn't simply adore me

enough to lead the group to please me. After relin-
quishing his leadership role, he began to miss Sunday
services, citing job demands or being tired. I was deeply
hurt again that he didn't simply love me enough to worship God to please me.

My attitude on Sundays was absolutely despicable.
Unchecked emotions would range from disappointment
to anger before I left for church, to bitter tears and
inability to engage in worship, returning home to avoid-
ance and silence.

For a while I was feeling sorry for myself, and I
prayed for God to touch my husband's heart and change
him. Surely, he wouldn't spend years in what I considered such a dangerous position. If I prayed hard enough,
I knew that God would honor me with a response to this
dreaded situation.

Friends at church began to tell me that they would
pray for the "prodigal" to return, but little did I suspect
that my husband wasn't the only one who had drifted
away from God. Although I was going through the
motions of being a Christian, my heart and motives
were far removed.

In January 2000 the proverbial rug was pulled from
under us. A routine physical examination revealed a
diagnosis everyone dreads. Cancer was present in my
husband's body, but no specific type of lymphoma had
been identified. This untimely event was a reminder of

his own father's early death with a cancerous tumor. What could we do now but cry and pray for a misdiagnosis or a deliverance from this tragic news.

I suppose that of the two of us I was the only one who prayed. Many fellow believers and friends joined me worldwide, but if my husband knelt in prayer, he didn't acknowledge it to me.

It was a year before the correct diagnosis of prolymphasitic leukemia came and a treatment plan had been decided by his oncologist.

It would take a miracle to pronounce him cancer-free after a year of treatments with devastating side effects. During his last round of chemotherapy, it was also determined by a routine checkup that prostate cancer was present. After the last poisonous IV line was removed from his vein, oncologist number two scheduled him for prostate surgery.

What a blow it was to realize that the disease could have the upper hand. Although six months later he was cancer-free and had generally recovered from the weakness caused by the chemotherapy and surgery, the miracle didn't come until much later.

Two years after being in remission with leukemia, we decided that a move to be closer to our children and grandchildren would be a timely event in our lives. Uprooting our lives after eighteen years in Georgia was extremely difficult, even knowing that this "well" time was a blessing from God. It was an opportunity for enriching family relationships and for making a home on the banks of beautiful Lake Texoma. Yet, I struggled emotionally, living in a pool of tears, parting from the friends we had made for a lifetime and from the church that had supported me with love and prayer through our time in the valley.

Looking back, I'm still ashamed of myself for doubting God's purpose in this move. Apparently, I had no vision of the great work the Almighty was prepared to do in our new life in Oklahoma.

I noticed a tiny church near our home as we navigated the curved, pothole-ridden road that led to our house by the lake. That would surely be my home church and my place of refuge with brothers and sisters to console me as I alone continued my walk of faith with God.

To my surprise, my husband dressed for services on that first Lord's day in our lakeside home. A ray of hope shone in my heart that morning, which became a bright, light-filled display of God's love and His perfect timing as we stepped through the doors of the church building to meet thirty wonderful, Spirit-filled people.

That Sunday morning as the Word was spoken, a genuine miracle occurred. My true belief in God was renewed and hope for the future glistened like the sun.

As I look at my husband preparing his lesson to

present to our Wednesday evening Bible class, I know for certain that God changed two hearts *upon* belief—a miracle that only He can do.

Miracles never cease!

A NOTE FROM THE EDITORS

This original book was created by the Books and Inspirational Media Division of Guideposts, the world's leading inspirational publisher. Founded in 1945 by Dr. Norman Vincent Peale and his wife, Ruth Stafford Peale, Guideposts helps people from all walks of life achieve their maximum personal and spiritual potential. Guideposts is committed to communicating positive, faith-filled principles for people everywhere to use in successful daily living.

Our publications include award-winning magazines like *Guideposts, Angels on Earth, Sweet 16,* and *Positive Thinking,* best-selling books, and outreach services that demontrate what can happen when faith and positive thinking are applied to day-to-day life.

For more information, please visit us online at www.guideposts.org, call (800) 431-2344 or write Guideposts, 39 Seminary Hill Road, Carmel, New York 10512.